Reading Tricia Lott Williford i
who is crazy smart but so warn
fascinated and not the least bit intimidated. Her perfectly-named new work is exactly the kind of book you want to press into the hands of others with a wink and a nod at the title. In *This Book Is for You*, Tricia leads us on a winsome journey through knowing, loving, and navigating the Bible, not as a know-it-all tour guide but as an empathetic fellow pilgrim. This book is for you. And for everyone you know.

MAGGIE WALLEM ROWE, speaker, dramatist, author of *This Life We Share*

I'm in absolute awe of what Tricia has created here. Whether you're new to studying the Bible or you've been doing it for decades, you'll come away from this book with a new love for the Scripture. This book is for you because *God is for you*. He craves for us to be people who understand the importance of learning to study his Word ourselves, not merely content on being spoon-fed the thoughts of others. Tricia writes in a magical way that makes you feel like you're simply having coffee with her. You'll come away understanding the hows and whys to studying the Bible in an attainable way. Grab a highlighter, friend—you're going to need it.

TERESA SWANSTROM ANDERSON, author of the Get Wisdom Bible Study series

Tricia is a trusted and winsome guide, taking us gently by the hand, inviting us to look into God's Word—either as a cynical longtime student or a curious bystander. What a delightful experience to have such a thoughtful guide to her beloved Bible. With the depth of a sage, she kindly concludes each chapter with practices for our actual life. This is a book you will underline and highlight. Read slowly and savor.

DON PAPE, curator of Pape Commons

This book is like a deep breath of refreshing air after a summer rain shower. It's not just a collection of real-life stories and relatable Scripture for each of us in today's spirit-oppressive environment. It's a how-to: how to fall in love with the One who first chose you—the intimate lover of your soul. We need his most excellent words of comfort, promise, and hope now more than ever. What an appropriate and wonderful double entendre title: *This Book Is for You*. Yep. On both counts. Tricia's short chapters and conversational writing style compel you to keep turning her pages for more. And her pages point you directly to *his* pages. The chapter-ending "Practice for Your Actual Life" personal-application exercises are spiritually eye-opening and perspectively game-changing. Highly recommend!

DEBORA M. COTY, speaker, award-winning author of the bestselling Too Blessed to be Stressed series

Winsome, warm, down-to-earth. Thanks to Tricia's wise and gentle guidance, I found my love for God's Word rekindled, and I didn't even think I needed a renewed perspective. I can't wait to share this book with friends and family all along the spiritual journey. No matter your past or current relationship with the Bible, Tricia's book is for you.

ANGIE WARD, PhD, assistant director of DMin at Denver Seminary, author of *I Am a Leader*

TRICIA LOTT WILLIFORD

This Book
Is for You

Loving
God's
Words

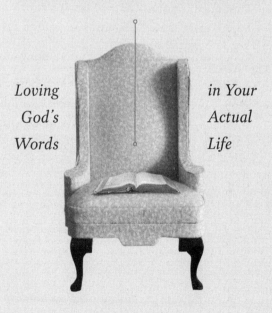

in Your
Actual
Life

A NavPress resource published in alliance
with Tyndale House Publishers

NavPress is the publishing ministry of The Navigators, an international Christian organization and leader in personal spiritual development. NavPress is committed to helping people grow spiritually and enjoy lives of meaning and hope through personal and group resources that are biblically rooted, culturally relevant, and highly practical.

For more information, visit NavPress.com.

OTHER BOOKS BY
TRICIA LOTT WILLIFORD

*And Life Comes Back: A Wife's Story
of Love, Loss, and Hope Reclaimed*

*Let's Pretend We're Normal: Adventures
in Rediscovering How to Be a Family*

*You Can Do This: Seizing the
Confidence God Offers*

*Just. You. Wait.: Patience, Contentment,
and Hope for the Everyday*

Contents

For anyone who has ever wanted to love the Bible,

but who has felt like it was written for someone else;

and in gratitude to every teacher who has

ever made the Bible come alive,

who has helped me fall in love with God's words in my actual life;

and for my young men, Tucker and Tyler.

May you grow in wisdom, in stature, and

in favor among God and people.

May you have the wisdom to know right from wrong,

and may you have the courage to do it—

even when it's hard.[1]

This Book Is for You

Hi. My name is Tricia, and I have not always loved the Bible.

I mean, I *wanted* to love it. I felt like I *should* love it. But I spent a lot of years of my life feeling like I was reading something meant for someone else.

That sounded like the opening sentence of a twelve-step program, I do realize. But I have a growing awareness of a tiny black pearl of a secret, and I suspect a lot of us are carrying it: In our private heart of hearts, many of us secretly feel like the Bible is boring. It seems to be irrelevant, questionable, meant for someone else living a much holier or more religious life than ours. That kind of secret doubt can make us feel like we need an anonymous support group fueling its members with acceptance and strong coffee.

Here's me raising my coffee cup. Cheers.

Perhaps that is not quite how you expected "a book about the Bible" to begin. Perhaps you are feeling right now that a book like this one should begin with stories about mission trips and sacrificial giving and spring-break fasting. But I've discovered that living and loving the Bible right where I am in my everyday life looks a little—or a lot—different from what we all may have expected.

I am not a seminarian, an academician, or a theologian; I am not a Bible teacher or even a Bible scholar. I am a lover of messy people, a tarbled mom of two teenage boys who are often late for school and wearing mismatched socks. My vacations are not called mission trips; I have been known to absentmindedly doodle in the margins of overdue library books; I have battled depression and anxiety to degrees that have nearly drowned me; I have begged the Lord for miracles that only he could provide; and somewhere in the midst of all of that, I fell hopelessly in love with the Word of God as a light for my next step and the air for my next breath.

So if you were hoping that a book about "loving God's words in your actual life" would open with a deep dive into the Pentateuch (or if you are actually looking for a book that tosses around the word *Pentateuch*), then please forgive me. And please (truly, *please*), do not go on Amazon to write a review about how you tossed this book into the trash because my writing voice sounds more like your friend than your Bible professor.

(That actually happened. It was a sad day that made me wish two things: (1) that my teenage sons did not enjoy reading my bad Amazon reviews aloud at the dinner table; and (2) that I was the kind of author who doesn't care to make friends with her readers.)

Here's the thing: *I am more like your friend than a Bible professor.*

I won't sound like an Old Testament scholar in this book. I mean, I probably could, if I tried really hard.

(Exceptionally hard.)

But I feel like there are enough books like that, written that way, with all those appendices and footnotes and small print. I've read many of them. I have passed exams about them. I have a deep respect for them, and I even like them. (Well, some of them.)

I'm just not here to write a book like that. Because, honestly, I think some of us may need a path to take a closer view of God's words that meet us right where we are. We don't need more information. We need community. We need inspiration. We need hope.

Maybe this idea, this path of reading the Bible and following Jesus, is new to you. Maybe you've kept your distance a bit from God and this book called the Bible because you're a bit wary of the people who follow him. Perhaps you've been deeply and personally wounded by Christians because I'm sad to say we have a long history of doing and saying truly terrible things in the name of Ignorance and Arrogance and groupthink.

If you find yourself there at the beginning of this book, please let me say: Those people were not following Jesus through that behavior that hurt you. Jesus was not—*is not*—ignorant, arrogant, or a shepherd of Groupthinking, asking us to do what everyone else is doing because it's accepted as the standard for what everyone has always done. He is—*and was*—an all-knowing, patient, gracious, question-asking, peacemaking, humble revolutionary. (He was not peacekeeping, however, because sometimes you have to get in a little bit of good trouble[2] on the path to making peace, and the Prince of Peace showed us this, indeed.)

Maybe a part of you, though, still wonders what it's about. This God, this Bible supposedly full of his words.

Or maybe you once knew a Jesus follower who intrigued you. And you wondered if that could be a path for you, but it seemed too different. Too much of a stretch. Too far from anything you have been taught, learned, known, lived.

Here's the part where I set down that coffee cup I raised a moment ago, where I lean in like a trusted friend, where I tell you this thing I want you to know: *This story is big enough for all of us, no matter where we come from or what we've gone through.* And this book of God's words tells us that he's not far from any of us.[3]

Maybe you're already in this commitment, though. You're an explorer, new to the Christian faith, and want to find your way through the Bible for the first time. You may be looking for some starter suggestions and a road map to begin the journey. My heart bursts with anticipation for you and all that you are about to encounter, my friend. Buckle up! Many have stepped onto this road over the years, and they found it to be life-changing in the most incredible ways.*

Or maybe you're in the group I like to call the "once-agains." You've been following Jesus for a while and have a basic understanding of the Bible—you can navigate your way through the table of contents and you know how to find Psalms and the stories about Jesus in the Gospels. You've listened to more sermons than you can count and you feel like you know what the Bible says, but you're bored with it. Maybe you'd like to fall in love with it because *you* want to, not become someone else told you to—and especially not because you have to pass a test at the end of this reading. Perhaps you're looking for some ways to ignite your fire again. Let's remember together what we once loved so much and seek new understanding, as well. Let's get to know more than the contents of the Bible—let's get to know the God of the Bible.

Or perhaps you may fall in the "want-to" category. You feel like you need to put a brown paper cover over this book because you've been hiding the fact that you've never really loved the Bible at all.

---

* If you're in that category, check out "Fifteen Things to Know as You Navigate the Bible" on page 154, where we talk about some easy ways to figure out all those books and references.

You *wanted* to love it.

You *intended* to love it.

And you so wish that you loved it.

But you just don't.

Maybe you don't enjoy reading much of anything, or perhaps you really love to read books—but not *this* book. Maybe you met Jesus a long time ago, but you never picked up your Bible back then, and now it seems too late to join the party that other believers seem to enjoy so much. Maybe you feel like everybody else already knows what you should have learned a long time ago. My heart is so tender for you, my friend. *You don't need to feel any shame or guilt in learning what you want to learn, at whatever life stage the knowledge finds you.* Let's dive into these pages together, where I promise you'll find joy, love, and life in abundance.

Or maybe you've thought this invitation to know him surely couldn't include you because you don't often feel invited or included. Because it's too much too soon, too little too late, too different and too exclusive, or—God, forgive us—too judge-y and too ugly. But no matter what your relationship with God and the words he inspired has looked like till now, here's what I want you to know.

(And here's where I need you to imagine me again, making eye contact, making sure you can hear me, making sure you are really, truly listening.)

You are holding this book in your hands. That means that I am inviting you, but far more important, God is inviting you. He has chosen you. Not because my particular book is a divine tool of any kind but because God can use anything he wants—from divine texts to absolute drivel—to get your attention. And if these first pages have pricked your heart, if you feel even remotely interested in falling in love with God's words in God's book, then I daresay that God is getting your attention.

He chose you.

He is choosing you right now, in this very moment of your actual life.

His book is *for you*.

○——————○

It is fun to be invited.

Invitations are the opposite of exclusion. They're not pushing you away or passively letting you wander by; when you're invited, someone is reaching out, pointing at you—*yes, you*—and saying, *This day, this table, this story, this time will not be the same if you are not part of it.*

I have a friend who, whenever she is planning an event at her house, intentionally invites more than she thinks will come, maybe more than her home can hold. When we met, I was newly widowed and transitioning from one church community to another, and all of my traditions and plans and sense of stability and belonging were up in the air. Kim was planning a party for Easter Sunday, complete with Easter eggs and an Easter egg hunt, and she called and said, "I don't know if you have any plans, but I wanted to invite you. Because isn't it fun to be invited?"

I have never forgotten the beauty of how she said that, how simple and how true.

You see, it doesn't take much for me to encounter the opposite of invitation, the kind of feeling that took root inside me the first day of middle school. I call it Cafeteria Syndrome, that visceral memory of standing in the cafeteria, holding my tray, not knowing where to sit. I have always hated that crippling fear of being left out, of not knowing where I belong, of wishing someone would tell me what to do next. I secretly loved assigned seats—even if I didn't like where I landed, at least I knew where to go.

I think most of us have that old familiar feeling lying dormant just below the surface, that inner middle schooler who just wants to be invited. By someone, nearly anyone. We want a spot at the cool table, an invitation to the premiere, our names listed among *Who's Who*. We want to be invited to the book club, the dinner party, into the important conversations in the room where it happens.[4] We want to make the team, to open the acceptance letter, to get the matching T-shirt. There's something deep within each of us, a longing to belong, to be wanted, to be known.

And yet, we also don't want to blindly follow just because somebody told us to. We are not so committed to belonging that we are willing to abandon our own sense of purpose and influence in exchange for a club membership.

I've read that "religion is for people who are afraid of going to hell, and spirituality is for people who've been there."[5] For a lot of us, a list of rules and guidelines and an "in or out" mentality are a stifling, suffocating personal hell. We're not into that.

When it comes to spiritual things, so many of us—especially in Gen X, the Millennial generation, and Gen Z—yes, we want to know that we're cared for, loved for who we are, and accepted where we are. But also, we are more hungry for *why* than *what*. We have a deep thirst for purpose, influence, and meaning. We want relationships, not rules. We want authenticity, not traditions. We want community, not clubs. After all, we have a deep suspicion of formulas and structured approaches to religion, and that's why we might not be so intrigued by Christians or Christianity.

And so we leave the Bible on the shelf, or asleep in the app on our phone, because we think it's a book of formulas and words written for people who know how to decode the secret language. If we're going to read anything, then we want to know it was written for us. And if we're going to read the Bible, we want to know that God and his Word are relevant, pertinent, and personal. We want to know if all this matters right where we are, in our actual lives.

When Jesus walked the earth in his public ministry, he often invited people into conversation with him. He ate dinner in their homes. He attended their weddings. He told stories they could relate to. He listened to the women who had been ignored. He welcomed the children who had been silenced. When Jesus spoke to people, he drew them in, right where they were. His invitations sparked such curiosity among the people who first heard his words that fishermen left their jobs, sons left their hometowns, and people followed this man just to see what he was about—and others stayed right where they were, in their jobs and circles and communities, now with a new, life-giving sense of direction. They were drawn to him, to everything he was about. Because he saw them and spoke about things that actually mattered to them. Because he loved them first.

Jesus was God before our very eyes, and the Bible is God's words right before our very eyes. And just like Jesus, the Bible loves us first, before we open its pages. The sacred pages are alive, and they invite us into a conversation.

No matter what we feel about Christians and the church, which so often can make us feel like that middle-school kid, wondering if there's a seat for us, this Bible full of God's words is itself an invitation for us to listen, to taste and see, to come along, and to follow. Jesus' most personal and direct invitations are buried well into the second half of the Bible, but even the sometimes-hard-to-understand Old Testament is the story of the grander invitation, of God inviting his people into relationship, of how he moved toward them again and again, even when they lost their way. The Bible starts with the story of an invitation, and then we get to Jesus and we discover the most delicious truth: *We are invited too.*

The Bible is a literary collection of books and letters, but it is also a living, organic text that contains echoes of the timeless and eternal voice of God. It is words on a page, but it is also a pathway to meet God. What if you could discover that the Word of God is alive, relevant, and for *you*?

I was sitting in a Bible class when I discovered that the woman near me, just two chairs away, was quietly dabbing her eyes with a tissue, hiding behind the curtain of her long blonde hair. We were classmates, we had spent many weeks alongside each other, but I only knew her name. I didn't know her story or why she was crying. At the whisper of an invitation to talk about what was on her mind, she came into the hallway with me, and she dissolved into a puddle of emotion. She was brokenhearted over her family, her kids who had wandered from church and home and love, and she was so sad that they didn't want to come to church with her.

I understood her heartache. As a mom who loves Jesus, there is nothing I want more than for my children to feel known, loved, and secure—particularly in the truth of Jesus Christ.

But as a Millennial, I also understood her kids. They didn't necessarily want to be in church with their mom on a Sunday morning. The young professionals and adults entering the world now want to feel seen and known for who they are, where they are, what they bring—not because they jumped through the hoops and followed the formulas set in place by generations who've come before. And, if we're honest, lots of how church has been done over the years is a lot of hoops and formulas.

Church is different now. It doesn't have to happen on Sunday morning, inside four walls. The process of studying, learning, and knowing the Bible can look and feel different too. Just because this woman's kids weren't learning in the traditional ways she had didn't mean they weren't learning. And this I know for sure: The God who made them was still pursuing them with his love. He doesn't need a building for that.

I assured my new friend that God is bigger than the will of our children and he exists outside the walls where she spends her Sunday mornings. I reminded her that it's our job to love our children, and it is our job to teach them, but it is not our job to change them. Only they are responsible for their choices. And I reminded her that God is bigger than anything we can imagine, his voice is alive in ways we can't wrap our minds around, and he is capable of reaching her kids in the way he chooses . . . and it may not be inside the walls of a church or a traditional Bible study.

She looked at me. A rivulet of mascara spilled down her cheek. And she said, "You really love him, don't you? You really love God. Like, really."

I was surprised by my own tears in reply. "I do. I really, really do."

And I've found him over and over again in the pages of his book.

We are invited—all of us—into this grand and beautiful story of God.

The story will not be the same if we are not part of it.

And now, he's inviting you to come along. Let him teach you. You're invited.

This book is for you.

Let's fall in love with this book—with this Jesus—in our actual lives.

CHAPTER I

Let's Start at the Very Beginning

Claiming a Posture

When I was a child, I had lots of tactics for that nightly window of sleeplessness, the long moments that stretched between "bedtime" and "actually sleepy."

I memorized the introduction music of *St. Elsewhere*, my parents' favorite medical drama that happened to coincide with bedtime. The fact that I can still recall the intro music likely means that I was interrupting the first few minutes of their weekly appointment with NBC's best lineup. (How parents ever effectively navigated the bedtime routine with any grace at all before the invention of the DVR is a theology beyond me. God bless the makers of pause-able live television and the umbrella of grace for the thousand nightly interruptions of the preschooler in violation of bedtime code.)

Sometimes I counted (again) the starry constellations of glow-in-the-dark stickers on my ceiling.

Sometimes I made my brother laugh from his bedroom across the hall with my uncanny impersonation of Ed McMahon. (Another glimpse into my parents' post-bedtime TV routines.)

Sometimes I played a tricky game of my own invention, stretching my body out of my bed, putting my head on the floor but keeping my legs and feet in the bed, thereby technically following my parents' mandate to stay in bed and "not let one foot touch the floor one more time, young lady." As I inched my head farther and farther away, I sometimes got too far away from my own feet and toppled to the floor like an overturned wheelbarrow of apples. And God help the child who makes that kind of ruckus while her parents are watching *St. Elsewhere*.

But most times, I lay awake trying to wrap my head around the concept of eternity. (Anybody else out there an existentially conflicted five-year-old? Just me? Great.) I imagined a long yellow brick road of time, unfurling like a ribbon in the directions before and after my life, never beginning and never ending. I imagined walking down that path as far as I could in either direction, left into the past and right into the future. From the very beginning to the very end. And it bothered me deeply to realize that even my greatest imagination could not wrap around a reality that big.

Never beginning? Never ending? Like . . . *never*?

I let myself explore as my mind dared, millions and billions of years. Sometimes it played like a VHS movie on rewind, going back and back and back in time, until I found this black vastness of outer space before anything existed, before anything was made. And in my imagination, there I found God, sitting by himself, in the dark, waiting to make something that could notice him.

That makes God sound needy, and I definitely don't mean to

imply that. God the Father, the Son, and the Spirit have existed as Three-in-One since the beginning of anything, and their relationship together is love exponential, spilling with the compounding overflow of fierce happiness. He already had love in this perfect three-in-one situation that is impossible for us to understand because it doesn't exist anywhere else. All we have to know is that God did not create humanity because he needed to be loved. He created people so he could share that love with us.

Anyway, I didn't get that yet when I was a sleepless little girl. I imagined him all alone, lonely, timeless, and bearded. (With exceedingly large hands.) I would lie in my bed and consider the fact that he had always been there, this Unmade Creator with no beginning. And I would get a little freaked out, feeling my heart beat faster, until it seemed wise to go back to counting the stickers on the ceiling.

Out of his bottomless love and creativity, he spoke light and he separated it from darkness. He spun spiraling galaxies sugared with more stars than we will ever discover, sprawling in directions and spanning distances that can only be measured in light-years. And of all the gazillions of spaces he created, he could have placed the human image of himself anywhere he chose. He picked this planet, this blue and green marble, as the palette for his imagination. He crafted thumbnail moon and blazing sun, ocean waves and powdery sand, green apples and blood oranges, daisies and tulips, giraffes and lime-green inchworms, eyelashes and freckles, songs that make your eyes water, and contagious laughter that makes your belly ache.

This God of the Bible has always been and always will be. Existence is his domain. Anything and everything find their life, meaning, and purpose. In him, we "live and move and have our being."[6] This will never not be true. God is vast and impossible for us to fully grasp, and the more I read his words, the bigger he becomes to me.

Here's one of the things that boggles my mind: Genesis wasn't written in the same season as it unfolded. It was written at least two million years after all that history had taken place. This opening book of the Bible gives us a glimpse of what happened, what God has done, and how he has interacted with his favorite creation since the first sun rose on the first morning. And since the first pen landed on the first page, people have been questioning who wrote it, analyzing the timeline, and arguing over who was really in charge.

People debate whether the week of creation happened in a literal week of seven days, or if the week is figurative language, a metaphor for a God for whom a thousand years are like a day.[7] Some don't buy it, don't believe it, consider it to be the vivid imagination of a writer for whom science did not yet exist. Honestly, does it matter how long it took? I just don't think that was the primary concern of whoever wrote the book of Genesis. (Tradition says that it was likely Moses, but we can't know for sure.)[8] I suspect he was less concerned with clarifying *how* God created the world, and far more concerned that generations to come understand *that* God created the earth. It happened, and God did it. All the specific details of how it happened are above our pay grade and capacity. Those fall under the category of "God Only Knows." What matters is our willingness to understand that God is vast and impossible for us to fully grasp—and therefore that the Bible is full of things we won't be able to 100 percent pin down. But that's okay. We get the freedom to not have all the answers, to have the humility to say it doesn't fully matter whether God created the world in seven days or whether that's a literary device, because what matters is that he did it.

Let's acknowledge that some of this stuff is hard to imagine, and if you're working to nail down proof before you'll step into faith, then you might have things backward. As I read the stories of the Bible, I am comfortable with the audacity, the unknowing, the question marks. I am less concerned with whether the remnants of Noah's ark can be found,[9] whether Job's travesties were literal or a parable,[10] whether Jonah was really in the whale for three slimy days,[11] or whether these are stories written to paint a picture and teach a lesson. To be clear, I personally choose to believe they happened as it is written, but that's because I generally tend to believe in things I can't understand when God is the One behind them, regardless. I choose to believe that he is who he says he is, and he is still mysterious, powerful, close, and loving whether everything in the Bible is literal or not.

So whether the world was formed in seven days or seven millennia does not change the Author of the story. I've decided I want to meet him in these pages, even if he shows up in ways I don't expect, even if he reveals himself in ways I don't understand. I want to trust him. Nothing about all of the debated pieces of the Bible can change the fact that I believe God is who he says, that he knows me and loves me, and that the greatest pursuit of my life is to know him and love him in return.

I want to know the heart of this God, and to become more like the One who authored this whole giant timeline that kept me awake at night as a child—and keeps me awake as an adult. Back then, I wanted to understand the timeline. Now, I am restless to know the One who invented time. I am hungry for more than information; I am thirsty for a transformation. I want to know this God who desires and delights in relationship, who values creativity and conversation, who created time but is never bound to the clock, who believes in rest even though he never tires. I want to know this God who has dominion over all things, yet knows my name, chose the color of my eyes, and recognizes my handwriting.

When God made his most prized and most privileged creation, man and woman, he made the first image of himself. When he created Eve—and I dearly love this discovery—he simultaneously created friendship and community, partnership and teamwork. He created the brushstrokes of love, affection, human connection. I want to know *this God*.

That's where we have to start with the Bible—not with our preconceptions, our biases, our understanding of different points of theology . . . but with God.

In my research for this book, I found this great guideline: "The main character in the Bible is God. As tempting as it may be to read these stories and ask, 'What does this tell me about me?' we must first stop to think about what these stories reveal to us about the character and nature of God. Otherwise, the stories become about the people of God instead of being about the God of the people."[12]

If you don't know whether you believe in God, if you're starting with the Bible and feeling uncertain because you don't know any of the things yet, then you're in really good company: God is beyond all of us. We all must have the ability to lay down our preconceptions of who he is, and we need to be willing to embark on a journey of discovery through his words. When we have a rightsized view of the mystery of God, we can approach the Bible with humility, curiosity, and open hands.

It's good to be amazed by something so much bigger than us. And, similar to my sleepless nights as a child, we might need to let ourselves get a little bit freaked out by how much we don't understand.

Practice for Your Actual Life

Write a list of everything you honestly believe about God right now. Not the stuff you "should" say, but who he actually is (or isn't) to you and what you think the Bible says about him. If you don't know at all how to feel about him or whether you believe in him, write what makes you curious and why you're picking up his book.

Resist the urge to tidy up your gut-level God-concepts. Even when it is messy, honesty is still a friend of intimacy with God.

ALICIA BRITT CHOLE, *The Sacred Slow*

CHAPTER 2

But Maybe Don't Start at the Very Beginning

Figuring Out What to Read

IT'S IMPORTANT FOR ME to tell you this up front: I'm so ridiculous I can hardly stand myself sometimes.

With that confession, this seems like a good time to sidestep into a mistake I made when I was teaching a room full of a thousand women about the Bible. Because stories of mistakes and embarrassing moments always make for great conversation, and I'm generally quick to break the ice by raising my hand to go first.

Now, I knew that a group that size would hold both ends and everything in between on the Bible-reading spectrum, from people who had read it cover-to-cover multiple times to those who were intimidated to open it. I wanted to connect with those who didn't know where to begin, to put a handle on the door to this "club" that can feel exclusive when you're on the outside.

So I offered them a few ideas on where to begin.

I said, "If you're starting for the very first time, open to the book of John. Jesus is the real deal, and that book will teach you who he was when he was here. The people who followed him found him straight up irresistible, and that book will show you why."

I still stand by that counsel, by the way.

Then I said, "Then, if you finish John and you're not sure where to go, open to James. I have a love-hate relationship with the book of James because it's a practical, hands-on approach to daily life. I love it because it's so easy to understand and I can't miss the meaning, but I also hate it *because it's so easy to understand and I can't pretend to miss the meaning.* So jump into James."

I still stand by that advice too.

But then I said, "Whatever you do, don't start at the beginning. If you start with Genesis and Exodus, then before you know it, you'll be in Leviticus and Numbers, and those long lists of laws can be a snore-fest. So do yourself a favor, and start in the middle."

I still stand by that too.

Except, when I finished teaching, the director of the women's ministry followed up with some announcements. She said, "And of course we'd like to invite you to our Women's Bible Studies, and, well, this is a little awkward after what Tricia just said, but we will be studying the book of Exodus. We do think that book is pretty interesting, actually."

I've now considered writing into the rider of any speaking-engagement contracts: "Please let me know what Bible studies you're beginning soon, so I can be careful which books of the Bible I disparage from the stage."

(Like I said: So ridiculous. Cannot handle.)

Now, here's where things get a little dicier for me in this whole embarrassing story. Yes, I thought the book of Exodus was boring . . . but that's because I hadn't read it for myself. It was on the list of things that I should have read along the way, books I'd learned about, attended classes for, seen on school syllabi, and even participated in discussions about . . . and had never actually read.

(This is a long list, I'm sorry to say. In addition to the books of the Bible, other things on that list include: *Catcher in the Rye. The Scarlet Letter.* Stuff by Flannery O'Connor. Basically anything I was supposed to read in high school, and a lot of what I said I read in college. There was a time when I could talk about them like I had read them. But I hadn't.)

The truth is, you can learn a lot from what somebody else says on a topic. You can even speak pretty intelligently without having done the work yourself. In my head, all of the happenings of the book of Exodus fit onto the flannelgraph of my childhood Sunday-school classes. The story of this guy named Moses and the people of Israel blends in with other things I was learning at the time, like the fact that my short haircut prompted my six-year-old peers to ask if I was a girl or a boy; or that the girl who sat beside me wore hearing aids; or that Psalms doesn't begin with the letter *S*. I was learning a lot of things back then, some interesting and some not, and somehow, the stories of Moses and Pharaoh and the Israelites and the Red Sea and the Golden Calf—they all got filed into a mental drawer labeled "Learned it: Not that interesting."

So, digesting that giant piece of humble pie, I decided to go back to my list of Things I Said I Read, and this time I actually read those early books of the Bible for myself. I started with the book of Genesis. And lo and behold, it came alive to me. I was deeply and surprisingly . . . *interested.*

What kept me from enjoying it before? Maybe it was the translation I had skimmed as my teacher read aloud. Not every version speaks your language—and I don't mean your native tongue. I'm talking about the language of your learning style, your approach, your preferences. If you're not reading a version that engages your heart, then pick a different one.

That makes it sound so easy, right? Like you just stroll into the bookstore, walk to the Bible section, and know intuitively which one is the one for you. The truth is, those shelves are filled with dozens of different English Bible translations, and it's enough to overwhelm the timid and send an overthinker right back to the car.

Let's clarify this first: There is no single "best" translation. Many people assume that there exists one Bible translation that is above all others, but there isn't. Writer and editor Mark Ward wrote, "You will save yourself some confusion and even heartache if you avoid aiming at this imaginary target, this holy grail. God never said there would be one best translation in any given language. And there isn't. Every Bible translation is the result of tens of thousands of small choices; it simply can't be that one translation got them all right and everyone else got them all wrong."[13]

So we can release our vice grip on getting this Bible-version thing right. For the most part, they all say generally the same thing in slightly different styles, so you won't find a Bible that says Jesus isn't the Son of God; or that claims cheating on your spouse is okay if you can justify how you met the person on social media and not in a coffee shop; or that tells the demoralizing tale of how Goliath killed David, not the other way around. You can't pick a wrong one. The only reason we have new translations is because language shifts over time and culture, so teams of knowledgeable people have come together to make the Bible interpretive and contemporary. It's not an easy process, and it doesn't happen quickly or lightly. But we can know that the translators of each version have agonized over how to convey the words accurately and consistently in a way that is both faithful to the text and meaningful to the reader.

Let's get playful with this, just a little. Imagine a long buffet of healthy breakfast foods. On the far left are the most proper of breakfast foods, and on the far right are the easiest to enjoy.

On the left, in kettles and pots from days of old, you'll find oatmeal, porridge, and such.

These are the biblical literary equivalent to the Lexham English Bible, the New American Standard Bible, the King James Version,[14] and the New King James Version.

In the middle, you'll find scrambled eggs and thick bacon, sliced to your liking as a meat eater. These are the New Revised Standard Version, the English Standard Version, and the Christian Standard Bible.

On the right, you might find a Denver omelet with sausage, ham, cheeses, red bell peppers, and onions, made to order. These colorful palates might be similar to the New International Version, the New Living Translation, or the New International Reader's Version.

On the far, far right, on pretty pedestals that are so lovely to look at, imagine colorful, layered yogurt parfaits that taste like decadent, fruity pudding. Here you'll find delicious paraphrases like Eugene Peterson's *The Message*.

(I hope you'll notice, none of these breakfast options loaded us up with carbs and empty sugars, like my beloved donuts or bagels with cream cheese. No, they're all great choices to start your day, hearty enough to carry you to lunchtime. And they allow others who enjoy their protein served differently to make their choice— but you both get good nutrition.)

When I relied on somebody else's teaching of the Bible's stories, I was settling for secondhand. I like how my favorite pink-haired theologian Teresa Swanstrom Anderson puts it: "Commentaries and books about the Bible are incredibly helpful, but we need to make sure we're not spending more time in books *about* the Bible than in the *actual* Bible," and "We must love the Bible in a way that surpasses others' opinion and research. To become spiritually literate, we must become a student of the Word."[15]

The reality is that I have been invited to the feast, and I was settling for crumbs off other people's plates. I let someone else do the studying, I let them read and enjoy the story firsthand, and I took the nuggets they handed me. When I started reading Exodus—and I mean, *actually reading it*, not reading someone else's interpretation of it, not reading stories about it, but actually turning to this second book of the Bible—I was captivated. The grit and fortitude of those Israelites. The foundation of redemption. My goodness, if I've ever been wrong about a book, I was wrong about Exodus.

(Now, Leviticus is still a little dry. But Leviticus is a contract. And just like the fine print of any contract, Leviticus can seem boring—unless you're one of those amazing individuals who loves to read every single word of a warranty. I'm not that girl.)

(Stay tuned for the verdicts on Flannery O'Connor.)

Practice for Your Actual Life

If you want to learn to enjoy coffee and you start with black coffee, it's bitter and difficult to drink. Likewise, if you start with Numbers and Leviticus, the Bible can feel bitter and difficult to swallow. Most coffee newbies do well to start by making their coffee taste nearly like a candy bar; then they gradually ease up on the sweetness. Choose your translation, and then dive into the book of John. That way, you can start with Jesus. He's the sweetest taste there is.

Some people find that they just give up because they get behind. Be willing to start a plan or ditch a plan depending on the context and your needs. Change from reading on a tablet to reading a paper Bible. Change from reading your Bible with verses; use the app to remove all the verse and chapter markings and just read it like a book. Listen to it instead of reading it. One way or another, let God's word soak into your life, soak into your soul.

TIM CHALLIES, QUOTED IN "HOW TO STUDY THE BIBLE: 9 TIPS FROM TOP BIBLE TEACHERS"

CHAPTER 3

Modern-Day Psalmist

Make It Yours

WHEN I WAS THIRTY-ONE YEARS OLD, my husband died on my bedroom floor. My sons were five and three years old, fatherless before kindergarten. The doctors thought he had the flu, but they missed a sepsis diagnosis, an infection in his bloodstream that attacked his heart and his lungs over just a matter of hours. They sent him home from the hospital to recover with Popsicles and Gatorade. They said, "He won't die from this, but he will feel like it."

He died the next morning. He was thirty-five and healthy, and he was suddenly gone. It was two days before Christmas, the eve of Christmas Eve.

If you and I are new to each other, I'm sorry to throw that curveball at you. It's a lot to take in, isn't it, that paragraph of raw facts? There isn't really a gentle or easy way to say it, to read the words on the page, or to hear them hang in the air. I know this well. That curveball hit my life with the velocity of an asteroid. It blew my world to bits.

If you and I have known each other for a while, if we have journeyed together through a book or two of mine, then you may be wondering if I'm going to tell the whole story again. Maybe you're wondering what more there is to say. These are fair questions.

I have learned many things, more than a decade after it all happened.

Some wounds become a scar that doesn't show. It doesn't bleed anymore, and it doesn't need the constant care it once required. Healthy tissue has been grafted over the scar, and sometimes even I no longer see it.

But it's there, part of the landscape of my life. Sometimes, during a hard rainstorm or a change of seasons, it feels tender once more.

I have had a lot of names in my adult life, and the long string of my first, middle, maiden, married, widowed, author, married-once-again monogram could make a bracelet long enough to wrap around your wrist twice. Every name of mine is like a nesting doll tucked inside the newest version. I am all of them together, and I am each, one at a time. At the very center is the smallest doll, tucked away, and all the other dolls work hard to keep her safe. She's in there.

I told you that I didn't always love the Bible. When Robb died, the Bible and I were not the best of friends. I didn't know what to do with it, this Old Testament that portrayed an angry God who let people die if they broke the rules, or this New Testament Savior who seemed to perform miracles only for people with enough faith. So, it could be said that either Robb died because we made

God mad, or he died because I didn't have enough faith to keep him alive.

Everything felt like too much or not enough.

I closed the Bible for a while, like an amateur athlete who hangs up her equipment. I didn't know how to use it, and I felt like I didn't want to learn. What good could it do now? I felt like it was my right to say, "No, thank you." If God was going to take away my husband and leave my children fatherless, then I was going to silence him for a bit. A long bit. He didn't keep his end of the deal, so I didn't intend to keep mine.

The word *entitled* comes to mind. I felt entitled to shut him out. Entitled to numb myself.

Entitled to take my questions elsewhere.

But here's what entitlement gives you: very little. You can "right" your way down the wrong path.

Everything felt empty. I remember trying to lose myself in a mindless novel, but I couldn't make sense of the plot, couldn't identify with these shallow characters. I remember trying to numb myself with the endless updates of social media, but I felt infuriated by a newsfeed of updates that were filled with inflated optimism or contrived crises. Once again, everything was too much or not enough.

At some point, I began to discover that I had nowhere else to go. And that triggered a memory buried deep inside my mind, of Jesus' friends coming to the very same conclusion. Jesus had said some very difficult things that most of his followers didn't want to hear. This life he had invited them to wasn't easy, shiny, or sparkling with wealth and popularity contests. They wanted something easier, and they began to turn away.

Jesus looked at the Twelve and asked, "You do not want to leave too, do you?"

And Peter, in his straightforward way that makes me love him so much, replied, "Lord, to whom shall we go? You have the words of eternal life."[16]

Peter didn't say, "I love every word you say." Or "This is easy to understand, and I have no questions." Or "I will never wonder or wander again."

Essentially, he said, "This is difficult, but I think it would be harder still without you. I would rather walk through this with you—and find meaning—than take another path that leads to meaninglessness, no purpose, no healing, and no life."

In my mind, I imagined Peter, weary in his eyes and tired in his bones, saying, "You're my only hope. Let's do this."

In his moment with Jesus, Peter answered for me too.

So I delivered my little boys to preschool, and I packed up my pens, my journal, and my Bible, and I went to Starbucks. I ordered my decaf grande salted caramel mocha, I took a spot at the corner table, and I waited. I waited for words. I waited for feelings. I waited for presence and goose bumps and inspiration. But just because I showed up didn't mean I knew what to say. The Bible still seemed so foreign to me, a treasure map I couldn't read.

I didn't want the Old Testament stories. (See previous point.)

I didn't want the New Testament stories. (See previous point.)

So I started somewhere in the middle. The book of Psalms.

The Psalms are a great collection of songs, poetry, and prayers written by many different writers, and together they reflect the heart, soul, and emotions of humanity. Martin Luther once said that this book "might well be called a little Bible," since it holds "most beautifully and briefly" everything that is in the entire Bible.[17] It felt like a good place to start.

I opened to the very first one, and I began to copy it into my journal.

I copied one psalm, then another. Then another. And I'll be honest—sometimes the words felt empty still. But the words gave me something to do with my thoughts; the copying gave me something to do with my hands; and the practice gave me something to do with my mornings.

And here's what I found.

I found prolific writers who cried out to God in the midst of real conversations in their actual lives.

I found writers begging God to listen.

O Lord, hear me as I pray;
     pay attention to my groaning.
Listen to my cry for help, my King and my God,
     for I pray to no one but you.[18]

I found writers in very real pain, wondering how bad this could get.

Have compassion on me, LORD, for I am weak.
     Heal me, LORD, for my bones are in agony.
I am sick at heart.
     How long, O LORD, until you restore me?[19]

I found people who were sleepless from crying.

I am worn out from sobbing.
     All night I flood my bed with weeping,
     drenching it with my tears.
My vision is blurred by grief.[20]

I found praise that was also a plea to God to keep his promises.

Arise, LORD! Lift up your hand, O God.
  Do not forget the helpless. . . .
But you, God, see the trouble of the afflicted;
  you consider their grief and take it in hand.
The victims commit themselves to you;
  you are the helper of the fatherless.[21]

I found poetry that was transparent despair, sistered with deliberate truth telling.

The cords of death entangled me;
  the torrents of destruction overwhelmed me.
The cords of the grave coiled around me;
  the snares of death confronted me.

In my distress I called to the LORD;
  I cried to my God for help.
From his temple he heard my voice;
  my cry came before him, into his ears.[22]

I found words I could claim in the darkness, even if I couldn't feel anything.

But as for me, I will trust in you.[23]

But I will keep on hoping for your help;
  I will praise you more and more.[24]

I found longing that said exactly what I felt.

"Oh, that I had the wings of a dove!
I would fly away and be at rest.
I would flee far away
and stay in the desert;
I would hurry to my place of shelter,
far from the tempest and storm."[25]

Over time, as I copied the psalms, I began to weave my words into theirs, adapting the psalms to become my own, becoming a modern-day psalmist in the pages of my journals. I would write the psalmists' words on the left side of the page, and I'd write my own on the right. I watched the pages turn, and I felt my heart soften.

How long, LORD? Will you forget me forever?
How long will you hide your face from me?
How long must I wrestle with my thoughts
and day after day have sorrow in my heart?
How long will my enemy triumph over me?[26]

How long do I have to do this?
How long will I feel this way?
Why did you let this happen to my life?
How long must I wrestle with my own thoughts
and every day have sorrow in my heart?
My enemies are depression, anxiety,
panic, and wrenching loss.
My enemies do not lurk with swords,
but they lurk in the darkness,
and they threaten to swallow me whole.
Is this okay with you?
How much longer?

Show me where to walk,
for I give myself to you.[27]

> Show me what to do.
> Show me how to do this.
> Show me.
> Be patient with me, please.

The LORD is close to the brokenhearted
and saves those who are crushed in spirit.[28]

> Jesus, I feel too tired to try.
> My days blend into one another.
> How is the next one different
> from the one before?
> My heart feels timid and afraid.
> It is hard to find courage when anything I try
> produces panic exhaustion.
> I am paralyzed.
> Be near. You said you would.

But I trust in your unfailing love.
I will rejoice because you have rescued me.
I will sing to the LORD
because he is good to me.[29]

> In your amazing love, you are
> holding me above bitterness.
> I have felt every shade of sadness,
> but I do not question your sovereignty.
> I feel a quiet purpose in this.

I do not feel like it is some horrifying mistake.
I have grieved the injustice of loss,
the unfairness of death.
But I have not believed you
to be unjust or unfair.
You have gifted me in many ways.
Two of these gifts are faith and discernment.
These are in full effect:
I believe you are on your throne,
and I believe there is purpose in your plan.
This is your grace.
This is your gift to me.

Hear my voice when I call, LORD;
be merciful to me and answer me.
My heart says of you, "Seek his face!"
Your face, LORD, I will seek.[30]

O Lord, how I hunger for you.
You have become the only
one I want to be with,
and I want to be with you for hours.
You are my safest place.
I have never known such
contentment in simply sitting.
Be still and know.
You are God.

The book is entirely void of clichés, which is maybe my favorite thing about it. As we read through the Psalms, we'll find writers saying the honest thing, not the easy thing. They are honest as they cry out to God from the deepest moment of their darkest night, and we will also find them honest as they sing in the heights of celebration.

This practice, this pouring out of words, doesn't guarantee healing or a softer heart. But it is a path to honesty. When we rely on empty words and recited phrases that we've repeated for decades, we limit our communication with God. Sure, he hears our words and he understands our attempts, but he longs for genuine communication. Since I am a longtime avoider of small talk, one who dives deep and fast, I like to think that our desire for authentic conversation is part of being made in the image of God. He knows us, and he wants us to know him.

I have learned this about God—he doesn't let us languish in monologues. He's a conversational God. As we learn to listen, as we speak out the words of our deepest pains and longings, eventually, we hear him speaking back. The path to any level of understanding must begin with honesty, and the psalmists pave the way. They show us how to tell God the truth about how we feel, what we've done, where we've been, what we love, and what we need. We can borrow their words until we find our own.

Practice for Your Actual Life

One of the great joys of my life is a writing workshop that I teach called *The Pen and The Page*. Writers of every age and stage come together, anyone who enjoys the art of chasing their thoughts on the page, and we explore the practice of writing as a way to understand ourselves better, to let our words find fresh life and meaning, and for many of us, to talk to God and let him speak over our stories. I call it worship. Every single weekend feels like a feast of new friendship, words, and authenticity. There is something magical that happens when the pen meets the page, and I believe that the Spirit of God shows up.

I teach this practice of exploring the Psalms and making them your own by looking closely at the beauty of Psalm 136. First, take a moment to read and reflect on this psalm:

Give thanks to the LORD, for he is good.
> His love endures forever.

Give thanks to the God of gods.
> His love endures forever.

Give thanks to the Lord of lords:
> His love endures forever.

to him who alone does great wonders,
> His love endures forever.

who by his understanding made the heavens,
> His love endures forever.

who spread out the earth upon the waters,
> His love endures forever.

who made the great lights—
> His love endures forever.

the sun to govern the day,
> His love endures forever.

the moon and stars to govern the night;
> His love endures forever.

to him who struck down the firstborn of Egypt
> His love endures forever.

and brought Israel out from among them
> His love endures forever.

with a mighty hand and outstretched arm;
> His love endures forever.

to him who divided the Red Sea asunder

His love endures forever.

and brought Israel through the midst of it,

His love endures forever.

but swept Pharaoh and his army into the Red Sea;

His love endures forever.

to him who led his people through the wilderness;

His love endures forever. . . .

He remembered us in our low estate

His love endures forever.

and freed us from our enemies.

His love endures forever.

He gives food to every creature.

His love endures forever.

Give thanks to the God of heaven.

His love endures forever.

Oh, my friends, these words get me every time. Do you see that bumpy road in the left column? This is not all sunshine and daisies, all good days to remind us that God's love endures forever. No, this God who paints the mornings and poured the oceans is the same Maker who divided the Red Sea into a walking path and swept Pharaoh and his armies right into it. He hung the moon and named the stars, and he remembers us in our darkest nights. *His love endures forever.*

Take a moment (or many moments) to imagine your own timeline. Imagine a long line from the left to the right, stretching across the horizon of your life. On the farthest left, the day you were born. On the farthest right, today. Let it play out before you like a movie reel of your best—and worst—scenes.

Make a list of your life's headlines. You don't have to go into detail; just use a few words you can recognize. Consider people who came in and out of your life, births and deaths. Write down a move into or away from communities that grounded you or wounded you. Include any marriages, their beginning or ending. Jobs awarded and eliminated. Wandering career paths and the mentors you picked up along the way. Health victories and losses, maybe some that only you and God know about. Consider each year of your life, and bring your timeline right up to this day.

And now, one headline at a time, write your psalm of praise to a God whose love endures forever.

This is what mine looks like, pulled from the season of Psalms and Starbucks:

I was born six days past the anticipated due date,
> on July 24, 1979.
>> *His love endures forever.*

Twenty-two months later, my brother was born,
My first friend and the sunshine of my life.
>> *His love endures forever.*

I had many teachers in my life, some who loved me,
> one who didn't.
>> *His love endures forever.*

I became a teacher, my life's goal.
>> *His love endures forever.*

I married Robb on July 22, 2000.
>> *His love endures forever.*

We lost our first child the day before Thanksgiving,
when there was no heartbeat on the ultrasound screen.
>> *His love endures forever.*

My first son was born.

His love endures forever.

We lost a second child during pregnancy.

His love endures forever.

My youngest son was born.

His love endures forever.

I stayed at home with my little boys, changing diapers
    and reading stories
and making lunch and folding laundry and feeling tired.

His love endures forever.

Robb and I nearly lost one another in the tyranny
    of raising small children.

His love endures forever.

Then we found each other again. Just in time.

His love endures forever.

Then he died in my arms.

His love endures forever.

It was so hard and so sad for so long.

His love endures forever.

The Lord became so real to me, my faithful companion.
I could not get enough of him. He is all I wanted.

His love endures forever.

He is near to the brokenhearted. He is close to those
    who are crushed in spirit.

His love endures forever.

In that original psalm, and in my adaptation, I discovered something: God's timeline continues, and his mercies to his people are a great continuendo from the beginning to the end.

How I wish I could sit with you and listen to your timeline, your headlines, your poetry. His love connects the dots from your constellations to mine.

His love endures forever.

The best moments in reading are when you come across something—a thought, a feeling, a way of looking at things—which you had thought special and particular to you. Now here it is, set down by someone else, a person you have never met, someone even who is long dead. And it is as if a hand has come out and taken yours.

ALAN BENNETT, *The History Boys*

CHAPTER 4

How Is This "a Future and a Hope"?

Understand the Promises

THE SMELL HIT ME IN THE FACE as soon as we stepped into our home. *Gross. What is that?* I mentally recalled the week's menu of refrigerated leftovers. Rotten potatoes? Old onions? Spoiled chicken? (Who are we kidding when we pack leftovers away? As my dad says, "Should we throw these out now, or should we put them in the fridge and throw them away next week?")

Something smelled awful.

I turned into a drill sergeant. "Everyone take out the trash. Any and all trash. Stat."

Every trash can was emptied, and the refrigerator had been purged . . . and still. The smell. Such an ugly smell. It could not be ignored.

At a loss, I went downstairs to the basement to find some ice cream to feed my feelings. (Mint chocolate chip, thanks.) One foot off the bottom step, I found the problem. My foot sank into the carpet with a sploshy squish.

The basement had flooded. That horrendous stench was from wet carpet and padding, swollen and saturated with standing water.

Fantastic.

I called our insurance company to get the wheels of bureaucracy turning in our favor. This burst pipe or faulty sprinkler—whatever culprit had ruined my basement—would not be my undoing.

While I was on hold for one of many phone calls, I started playing the mental game I rely on in moments like this one. It's called *If I Liked Something about This.* I learned it from an art professor in college who utilized this strategy for teaching students to assess art. "You don't have to like this painting, but if you liked something about it, what would it be?"

If I liked something about this situation of a ruined, flooded, rotten basement:

. . . I would like the fact that the subfloor under all of this mess is a cement floor, not particleboard, like so many basements in our part of the country.

. . . I would like that I listened to the tug on my intuition last week, that little whisper that said, *You know all those boxes of books from your publisher, your entire inventory of titles written by you, that are sitting on the floor downstairs? Think about moving those to a safer spot.* (And thankfully I had done more than "think" about it.)

. . . I would like that this is a great opportunity to Marie Kondo the basement. I mean, it's humbling to navigate the excess of so many Nerf guns, school yearbooks from the 1990s (or 1970s, for one of the people in this marriage), the holiday wreaths, base-balls, cowboy hats, outdated college textbooks, a decade's worth of Christmas wrapping paper and ribbons, manuals for every kitchen appliance we've ever had—and some we've never had—and most surprisingly, four actual trombones. (Insert all the question marks.) So yes, indeed, if I liked something about this mess, I would like that I've been presented with this opportunity I would not have chosen.

. . . I would like that I have insurance. In moments like these, that monthly payment is an easier pill to swallow.

But then the insurance company spoke into the madness. This damage was not from a faulty sprinkler or a burst pipe. It was the result of a torrential hailstorm.

Ah, yes. I recalled that hailstorm. The boys and I had been fin-ishing up some after-school errands when that monster unleashed. I drove home through it. Tyler had captured video on my phone of the cars hydroplaning, the ice piled on my windshield, and the puddles that nearly swallowed our car in giant waves. Yes, I recalled that storm.

So while I was hunched over the wheel with my hands at a solid ten and two, just trying to get us home before an ark appeared, the window wells were flooding and spilling into my basement, saturating everything but the trombones.

Here's a little insurance lesson for you. Did you know that if the cause is not within the house; if it is not the fault of wiring or pipes or sprinkles; if the cause is weather related and the result of biblical-scale rain—did you know homeowner's insurance does not cover that damage? I learned this on that day.

They called it "an act of God."

Let's just pause with that phrase for a moment. Because this particular word choice plunged my two teenage sons into a theological conundrum.

"So, you're telling me," they said, "that God allowed this storm. And he allowed it to flood our basement. And he's allowing this insurance company—whom you have paid every month—to say they don't have to help us because it was God's idea in the first place?"

(They may or may not have used the word *whom* correctly. Naturally, I choose to recall that they did. A girl can dream.)

Well, each of those statements seems to be true. So, yes. Apparently that's how this is going down.

Without insurance, there was nothing to do but get to work. The job was huge and daunting. We were on our hands and knees with work gloves and industrial carpet cutters, tearing this giant mess into strips that could be rolled and carried up the stairs and outside. We were soaked with water and sweat. The carpet reeked, and so did we.

It was during one of these sweaty, heavy trips up the stairs that my son Tucker said, "How is this 'a future and a hope'?"

He was quoting words from the Old Testament book of Jeremiah, chapter 29, verse 11: "'For I know the plans I have for you,' says the LORD. 'They are plans for good and not for disaster, to give you a future and a hope'" (NLT).

Tuck has asked me this question in other poignant moments where things seemed more than a little sketchy. Once, in the hospital emergency room, laid up with an asthma attack that got ahead of us, he lifted the oxygen mask off his face to say, "God made my lungs this way? How is this 'a future and a hope'?"

Many evenings between bedtime prayers and my official finish line for the day, he would slow down the whole routine with a dialogue that began with an earnest question: "God let my dad die before he could see me play baseball. He could have let him live. How is this 'a future and a hope'?"

Each time, I tried to assuage his questions with the answers other people had given me. "Honey, that future and hope are still to come. He was talking about the life after this one. The hope of our salvation, the promise of our future with him in heaven. The good things don't always happen here and now, but we can still believe this verse is true."

On this day, I could tell my answer meant little. He was silent as he carried another giant load of dripping mess up the stairs.

Because when you're sweaty and wet with stink, words mean very little.

○————○

When we cherry-pick words (and rules) from anywhere in the Bible, it leads to bad theology. It makes everything harder and more confusing. Sometimes, we create almost-Scriptures that are downright dangerous.

For example, "God helps those who help themselves."

Did you know that isn't in the Bible? It's one of those almost-Scriptures, almost-truths that sounds like it could be from the book of Proverbs. People toss it around like it has a chapter and verse reference. Like "God won't give you more than you can handle."** Or "Cleanliness is next to godliness." Or "God hates quitters." All of those: Not true, and God never said them.

Then there are the statements that are true, but we use them as weapons against each other. Like "God hates divorce."[31] I mean,

---

**Many of us have had teachers and well-meaning advisors point us to 1 Corinthians 10:13, which says, "God is faithful. He will not allow the temptation to be more than you can stand. When you are tempted, he will show you a way out so that you can endure" (NLT). This verse promises that he will give us a chance to flee the things that tempt us, not that he won't give us more than we can handle.

I'm sure he does. Of course he does. Anyone intimately acquainted with divorce hates it. It's brutal and biting, destructive and heart-breaking. But I wonder sometimes if the end of a marriage belongs on a long list of things that he hates because they damage something he created. Sometimes we proceed as if some rules are written in all caps, as if they trump all the others. Our words might be born of good intentions, but they're delivered poorly.

Not only is God bigger than us but the Bible is bigger than us. There's a larger context and story for every story and verse. Often we misunderstand the Bible as a whole because we make it a book of simple clichés or isolated stories that we pull out of context to try to make sense of our lives. But there's a cohesiveness to the Bible that makes it so much richer and bigger. The Bible goes beyond how we want to use it, and while God graciously uses it to speak into our lives, we are part of a much bigger story. Ultimately, all these words and stories and the whole grandness of it all—it's all about him.

In the throes of a flooded basement, I opened the book I was reading: *Irresistible* by Andy Stanley. (Oh, this book; I want to give it to everyone who has a Bible or even a single question about how the Old Testament can say the things it says, mean what it means, and have any relevance for us today.)

Andy helped me—and I feel like I can call him by his first name because that's what I do with writers and teachers who have taught me so much. He helped me to understand that although the Bible is all inspired and all true from the first word to the last, it is not all equally authoritative.

One of the things I learned from Andy is that "testament" (as in Old Testament and New Testament) means "covenant"—which means that the Bible is made of an old covenant and a new covenant. As Andy said, "The fact that someone chose to publish the old covenant with the new covenant in a genuine leather binding doesn't mean we should treat them or apply them the same way. The Bible is all God's Word . . . to *somebody*. But it's not all God's Word to *everybody*."[32]

I won't say nobody ever taught me this distinction between the two parts of the Bible, but I can say that it never landed with this clarity until I was in the fourth decade of life and learning. (And by "fourth decade" I mean my forties, which I do realize is technically the fifth decade, but please kindly leave me alone about this.)

That's why you might find the Old Testament hard or confusing or weird. It's not your covenant. Sure, read for the history and awareness of how we came to the covenant we have now. And even better, read it for a deeper appreciation for the New Covenant and the New Promise and the fact that we don't have to eat our burgers without cheese,[33] we can change the toilet paper roll as needed—even on Sundays,[34] and we are allowed to wear cotton-linen blends.[35] And most of all, read to wrestle with the mystery and majesty of a God who wanted a relationship with his people, and his grief and pain when they walked away from that relationship.

But the implications for your life aren't black and white, an easy application of the literal reading devoid of the larger context. As Teresa Swanstrom Anderson notes, "The Bible was written for us, but it's not written *to* us."[36]

Even for the Israelites, the old-covenant words weren't necessarily right for them in that very moment. That promise in Jeremiah 29:11 wasn't an immediate fix for them; their future and hope wouldn't come about for seventy years. In those decades in between, most of the people waiting would die, and those who survived the Long Wait would experience exile, separation, grief, and heartache that we can't imagine. (Or pain that some of us can imagine, but to stare down such pain in light of the promise that it would last for seventy years . . . not very hopeful.)

Armed with this new understanding in the wake of our personal flood, I was excited to bring it up the next night at the dinner table. "Tuck! I am so excited to tell you what I learned! You asked me about that verse that talks about God's promise of hope and a future—and I learned that's not a promise for us anyway. That was his promise to the Israelites, not us."

I looked at him expectantly, waiting to witness his light bulb moment. He was not quite as enamored as I was by this discovery and distinction. Nonplussed, his voice flat, he said, "Okay, well, I'd rather have their promise than the one we have."

The kid raises a good point—and a good question.

The promise of the Old Testament sounds a lot more inviting than the promises of the New Testament. I mean, there's a reason why all the Christian-adjacent Etsy stores are flooded every spring with plaques and signs and bookmarks of Jeremiah 29:11. These words, taken out of context, are far prettier and feel more hopeful than the promises of the second half of the Bible, which say things like "In this world you will have trouble. But take heart! I have overcome the world."[37]

Take heart. It's hard to take heart in the overcoming when things are so wrong in your world, whether it's because the man cave flooded or because of far greater troubles, like people dying from a pandemic. "Take heart" is not my go-to. Is this gospel really Good News? Do I really want the promise that's before me?

These questions are the real of the real. My young man made me dig for answers. He wasn't going to lay this down without some truth. (When you teach your kids Scripture, they will quite possibly use it against you.)

We can be thankful for the new promise—our promise—because it doesn't require the death of our pets every time we do the wrong thing. Now we can ask forgiveness. Back then, anytime you broke a law, you had to kill something or burn something.

The new covenant is a promise to individuals who choose to follow Jesus, not a whole nation. It means I get to make a choice. I get to talk to God myself, not depend on priests and generations of rules. The promises found in most of the Old Testament are not promises to us, but the promises to us are better. As Andy said, "They may not be as promising, but they are better promises."[38]

When Jesus replaced the old covenant with the new, he replaced six-hundred-plus laws with one: LOVE. "As I have loved you, so you must love one another."[39] In fact, the only thing that matters now is faith that shows itself in love.[40] It means I get to know the Holy Spirit, the Spirit of God who lives within me, who didn't show up on the scene until after Jesus left. Nobody can know the most private thoughts except the person who thinks them. Nobody can know the thoughts of God except God. But get this—the Holy Spirit, the One who knows the thoughts of God, is alive within me, a gift I received as soon as I decided I wanted to know this Jesus, that I wanted to live a life pleasing to him. The Spirit can share with me the thoughts and insights of God. *I can know this God.*

When we try to fit the Bible into boxes that fit our lives and our stories, we forget that this is a way bigger story—and way richer than we realize. When we hold onto clichés we pull from the Bible, and when we take common shortcuts with verses, we can miss the richness of what God was actually doing.

This God is for everybody.

Any person.

All the people.

Anybody who's interested in participating.

We can know this God.

Practice for Your Actual Life

We have the privilege of the Bible in its entirety in our hands, but the first readers didn't have access to the whole thing. They had one book at a time. They had to read the information within the context it was given to them, and sometimes we forget that.

When Paul wrote a letter to a church of Galatians (one of Paul's letters to a church in the New Testament), they could not flip over to Revelation (John's vision of God at the end of time) to understand Galatians better, because Revelation had not been written yet. They couldn't even read Paul's letters to other New Testament churches in order to help them understand what he was saying in their letter to them.

In the book *Christ from Beginning to End: How the Full Story of Scripture Reveals the Full Glory of Christ*, Trent Hunter and Stephen Wellum remind us about the Bible, "Since it's a long book and pastors preach out of different sections each week, we get used to entering and exiting portions of Scripture without considering the context of the books in which they are found, let alone their location in the rest of the Bible's storyline . . . but this practice can . . . reinforce our tendency to read passages in isolation."[41] The Latin root *con* means "with," so *context* means "with the text." It's important for us to investigate: Who said it? When? Context is absolutely critical to understanding Scripture, and the Bible has several contexts to consider: historical context, cultural context, and literary context. It matters.

This is why one of the best ways—not the only way, but one of the best ways—to study the Bible is book by book. It's the way the Bible was written, and when we read one book at a time, we can read the content within the context. When you're stuck, reach out to online commentaries, dictionaries, and other resources to get the full context of the passage you're reading.

Personal Bible reading ought to have oomph to it. If you don't understand something, there's nothing wrong with taking a commentary off your shelf so that you can understand the passage better.

D. A. CARSON, QUOTED IN "HOW TO STUDY THE BIBLE: 9 TIPS FROM TOP BIBLE TEACHERS"

CHAPTER 5

After the Earthquake

Unbuilding to Rebuild

WHEN MY BOYS WERE SMALL, we were up to our necks in the Lego scene. The sun rose and set around their Lego creations on the floor, on the coffee table, in the bathtub, and sometimes even in my pillowcase. My sons were builders.

I remember when they would build something big and tall and glorious, a tower of their own making. "Look, Mommy. Look how strong and tall my _____ [spaceship, castle, tower, etc.] is!"

And then Molly, our chocolate Labrador, would pick up on the excitement in their voices, and she'd walk by and wag her tail, and the whole structure would start to sway. Panic would ensue as they rushed in to make repairs.

From my taller and wiser vantage point, I might say something like, "Hey, pal, what if you . . . maybe you need to . . . ," but my young builder would say, "No! Mommy! Don't touch it! I made it! *Don't touch it!*"

"But it's going to crash, honey."

"This is what I want it to look like, Mommy. Don't touch it."

"I won't touch it. I'm just making a suggestion. If you build a broader base over here, or maybe if you add some pillars over here . . . " Essentially, I was saying, "If you are willing to deconstruct this and build a firmer foundation, this is going to be even better later on."

Sometimes, when you look again at what's holding things up, you find the wobbles and the lack of support and the pieces not quite connecting. Sometimes, rebuilding makes the whole structure stronger.

Sometimes we must unbuild in order to rebuild.

I've built some wobbly structures to house my belief systems, you guys. I mean, I felt like they looked good on the outside, but essentially what I had was a house of cards, ready to topple over on a breeze. I couldn't see the flaws in my construction, and it made me very uncomfortable when anyone questioned what I'd built. *If this isn't solid, if this falls down around me, then what have I spent all this time building?*

Take a look at the life map I had constructed, for example.

I had a solid start on Christianity—I "asked Jesus into my heart" when I was three years old. I faithfully attended a large and impressive church, and I became a leader in my youth group. I went on mission trips for six consecutive summers, I was a camp counselor for all of my college summers, and I stayed on the straight and narrow path. (No alcohol or drugs for me, thanks. I was a good girl.) I was honest and obedient, and I memorized verses from the Bible and journaled through all of my emotions. I tithed ten percent of the money I made to God, and I was a virgin on my wedding day.

(Well, my first wedding day.)

So when I turned thirty, and things were moving right along as planned, I thought God had given me this life I had asked for. I actually thought I was an example of his favor for a life well lived, a reward in exchange for my three decades of obedience. I thought he had been so kind to me because he loved me so much. After all, he's a good, good Father who works all things for the good of those who love him.

Put a bow on this, I thought.

Obey God, and he gives you the life you want, I thought. Smooth all of that with a frosting theology of grace to cover any mistakes in my math, and you've got yourself a formula for God's favor and faithfulness.

It wasn't just that I thought $A + B = C$. I had created some sort of complex algebraic formula, where, if you compute all the factors . . .

SS = Solid Start	O = Obedience
CA = Church Attendance	V = Virgin on my Wedding Day
YG = Youth Group	SM = Scripture Memorization
MT = Mission Trip Every Summer	T = Tithe
	G = Grace
SN = Straight and Narrow Path	S = Strong
H = Honesty	J = Journaling

$$F^2 = 10\left(\frac{V\left(\left[SS + \left(CA^S + YG\right)^{MT^4}\right] + [SN(SM + J)]^{HO}\right)}{T}\right)^G$$

. . . you get F^2 = Faithfulness and Favor.

You guys.

That's absurdly difficult. Get one single factor a little bit off, and you've lost your equation for Faithfulness and Favor.

And also that's legalism. Legalism is the personal hell we create for ourselves when we rely excessively on moral laws, rules, and formulas. That's what we get when we turn a welcoming invitation into a checklist of rules to keep and follow.

I'm exhausted just looking at it. No wonder I was weary from living it. I tried to do all of it—obey his commands, seek justice, love mercy,[42] and all the rest of the long list of things he's asked me to do.

And trying to do everything right didn't "pay off" for me—because I had misunderstood the Bible, and I had misunderstood God. My formula for favor was actually an algorithm for a great unraveling. Robb died, and I came undone—big time. On the morning Robb died, everything fell apart in a soul-shattering earthquake.

There are smaller shakes that happen after large earthquakes, and seismologists call them "aftershocks." Aftershocks can be just as dangerous as the original earthquake because they are unpredictable and ongoing. Worst of all, they can continue for weeks, months, and even decades after the main quake. In general, the larger the mainshock, the larger and more numerous the aftershocks, and the longer they will continue. It's deeply unsettling.

Deconstruction is what happens in the middle of spiritual aftershocks, when what we thought we knew about life comes right up against what feel like contradictory realities about God. Deconstruction feels unsafe and scary, and the trouble is many of us find ourselves in relationships and communities where questions feel unsafe too. We shut down the dialogue, as if our faith is a house of cards. As if God is worried by the question marks in our thought bubbles. The world shakes, but we try not to pay attention.

But if we're willing to brave this kind of unbuilding, we're going to have to take apart what we have believed or understood about God. Maybe all the pieces might fit together in a different way, or maybe we're missing pieces altogether, or maybe we picked up some of the wrong pieces in the first place. Someone who is unbuilding might say, "I no longer believe what I may have believed in the past, and I'm trying to figure out which parts of my faith are really part of my foundation."

This process feels particularly alarming to me when someone I've studied under, or someone I'm close to—a friend or a mentor— goes through it. I find myself thinking, *You've given me some of my greatest moments of clarity. You've guided me to some of the anchors of what I believe in. What do I do if you're deconstructing them? If you're taking them apart, then it feels like you're taking me apart.* It feels like my foundation is shaking. And maybe it is.

But the truth is, living with a faith that is static and unmoving doesn't leave room for God to be who he is. We aren't all-knowing people. Some of what we were taught, or what we have believed, very well could be taking us away from him rather than closer to him. In the midst of the scary noise, there's a deeper reality: We have to unbuild in order for our faith to grow.

When my boys' Lego towers threatened to topple over, I had a few suggestions for my young builders. Essentially, I was saying, "If you are willing to deconstruct this"—well, perhaps I used one-syllable words that they knew, like "take it down"—"and build a firmer foundation, this is going to be even better later on. I have a little more life experience to see; all you need is this one other thing."

God, in his greatness, whispers to me, "Trish, it's okay. What you have is very beautiful. I'm just asking you to take what you've continued to learn about me and renovate your foundation."

In a mysterious and wonderful way, the Bible is our best comfort and guide in the midst of unbuilding. It's full of people asking hard questions, over and over, and God meeting them there. Goodness, the whole book of Job is a process of a man examining his faith and asking hard questions. He raised questions about God and pain that have baffled dinner parties and Bible scholars for centuries. Job's friends refused to budge in their preconceptions about God and how he works when we're hurting. But God blessed Job for wrestling through his biggest questions instead of accepting cliché, pat answers.

Here's the beauty of the Bible, though: Sometimes the answers are in there, even though they're not as black and white as we might want or expect. God doesn't answer every question, but he does progressively reveal deeper truths about himself and how he's working throughout his Word. When we start really diving in, and finding more of the pieces throughout, we can see that each of Job's questions is answered in the presence, existence, and life of Jesus.

- Job asked, "Is there someone who can help me approach God? If only there were a mediator between us, someone who could bring us together."[43]
- Paul answered in his letter to Timothy: "For there is only one God and one Mediator who can reconcile God and humanity—the man *Christ Jesus*."[44]

- Job asked, "Is there life after death? If someone could just tell me, this would give hope through all my years of struggle, and I would eagerly await the release of death."[45]

- Martha asked similar questions when her brother died, and Jesus told her, "I am the resurrection and the life. Anyone who believes in me will live, even after dying."[46]

- Job asked, "Is anybody in charge who is on my side? Is there anyone who has access to God, who might represent me?"[47]
- We find the answer in the book of Hebrews: "For Christ did not enter into a holy place made with human hands, which was only a copy of the true one in heaven. He entered into heaven itself to appear now before God on our behalf."[48]

- Job asked, "Is there one who can save us?"[49] Essentially, this time he answers his own question: "But as for me, I know that my Redeemer lives, and he will stand upon the earth at last."[50] Even though he couldn't see God's favor in that moment, he chose to believe God was ultimately on his side.
- And we find this answer later on in the Bible: "Because Jesus lives forever, his priesthood lasts forever. Therefore he is able, once and forever, to save those who come to God through him. He lives forever to intercede with God on their behalf."[51]

When we are reading the Bible in our actual lives, when we begin to see the whole story and understand that we're not just looking at disconnected fragments, we begin to put pieces together that cause us to think, *Oh, wait. I believed something that Jesus never really said in the first place*, or *I didn't know the answer was right there*. In the unsteadiness of unbuilding, the Bible is a rock we can lean on.

We all have seasons where we must unbuild our faith in order to rebuild it. It's normal. We can't stay immobile when something challenges our beliefs. We can feel shaken by any number of instabilities, like the end of a relationship we thought was "the one," or a job loss that leaves us reeling with questions and bills. Our foundations can feel uprooted by the questions of our insecurities (*What if I do not have what it takes?*), our fear (*What if I lose what has defined me?*), and by pride (*What if I'm wrong?*). Nothing quite challenges our faith so suddenly and sharply, though, like a crisis, when life takes a sharp left turn. Suddenly our experiences make us wonder if maybe God doesn't love us or isn't always there for us. The pieces fall apart, and we're left trying to reassemble.

In these great unravelings, we ask questions like, *Did I do something wrong? Am I being punished? Is Satan attacking me? Is there something in this that's supposed to prepare me to love others? Have I been specifically chosen for this test, like Job? Am I responsible for this? Or is this just something that happened?*

If anyone gives you a bulletproof answer to any of these questions, if they are so sure they know the answers that they've stopped asking hard questions, be very suspicious. The best answers I can find for suffering always come back to the word *maybe*.

Did I do something wrong? Maybe. Start by confessing any sin that comes to mind, but don't try to invent some sin if God isn't clearly showing you what you did wrong. In my experience, I know when I've done the wrong thing. I can lie to myself for a while, but in the end, I know when my heart is pricked with conviction.

Am I under spiritual attack? Maybe. You can ask God to strengthen and protect you. In my experience, I've learned to watch him rescue me in ways I didn't expect. It doesn't always mean the storm stops; sometimes it means he sends someone with a flashlight and an umbrella.

Is this supposed to prepare me to love other people better? Maybe. You can ask God to help you discover others who suffer as you do, but know this: Your loss does not have to become a ministry.

Have I been specifically chosen for this, like Job? Maybe. Accept help from people who love you, and like Job, choose to trust that God is on your side. Choose to trust.

Am I responsible for this? Maybe. But we live in a broken place of good and evil. Someday the suffering will end, but for now, this is what we have. Don't withdraw from God because you want to withdraw from the pain; God won't go away, and neither will the pain. Keep asking.

Hebrews 11, known as the Hall of Faith, describes how people following God through the ages had to trust—even when what was happening didn't make sense. The author says, essentially, that even when these people died, they hadn't received what they were hoping for because they were looking toward their home in a different place. They kept their eyes on something that could not be achieved here on earth. And through that tension, they chose to cling to God. In all of our unbuilding, as our foundation feels like it's shifting beneath our feet, we can cling to God when we don't understand anything else. And as we do, our faith will grow in valuable and necessary ways. We don't grow in comfortable answers, in stasis, in keeping the status quo. If we are unwilling to ask the hard questions—and if we are unwilling to sit with the people who are brave enough to ask—then our faith stays very shallow, and ultimately vulnerable.

If you are unbuilding, find someone to walk through it with you. Find many people. Seek out godly mentors, Christian counselors, people who love you and love God. Pour out your heart to the Lord, and stay in the Scripture, and don't be in a hurry.

Choose one book of the Bible at a time to read, keep reading, and read again. Read it in every translation on a Bible app. Read the footnotes and commentaries and cross-references. When you settle into just a few pages at a time, when you let them wash over you as you immerse yourself again and again, answers have a way of emerging.

In my own unbuilding, I had a team of women who stayed very close to me, and my family stayed close—even when I scared them. I think sometimes they were concerned about my decisions and my questions, and the freedom I felt to ask, do, and feel. They probably thought, *Who is this person? We could trust her before. What if she flies off the handle and doesn't come back?* But I needed that long leash. Leave me be, and let me grow. In asking questions *of me* as they walked *alongside me*, they held the string to my kite, and they didn't let me fly away.

The hard questions are not unanswerable. Sometimes they take us to more questions that point us to answers. When you depend on a formula, you have put God in a box. When that formula breaks, you meet a bigger, stronger God who doesn't need boxes at all.

Keep asking. Keep reading. Keep building.

Practice for Your Actual Life

Consider your own unbuilding. What were the weaknesses in things you once believed? How have your questions strengthened your view of God?

Or maybe you're not there yet. Maybe you're still tearing down and rebuilding and this whole thing feels deeply unsettling and alarmingly unstable. Allow yourself the space to ask the hard questions, to trust in a God who is big enough to live outside the boxes we put him in.

- I used to think this:

- Now I believe this:

Scripture is the most valuable commentary on Scripture, especially as we watch people change their choices, change the rules,
change their worship style, change their *minds* as they learn more.
As you read and mark up your Bible, you may find God reminding
you of similar verses and passages and truths that bring clarity of
explanation to your questions. Make notes to yourself, and get into
the habit of recording or highlighting these other parts of the Bible
that give you additional insights into what you have read.

I have come to believe that periods of struggling and doubt are such common experiences of faith, including in the Bible, that something is meant to be learned from such periods, however long in duration they might be.

PETER ENNS, *The Sin of Certainty*

If our theology doesn't shift and change over our lifetimes, then I have to wonder if we're paying attention.

SARAH BESSEY, *Out of Sorts*

CHAPTER 6

When I Didn't Know

Discovering the Only Rule That Really Matters

ONCE UPON A TIME, I decided to attend a small, conservative Christian college with a dress code and a curfew.

If you and I were playing a game of Never Have I Ever (which is perhaps customarily a drinking game, but I have found it to be just as effective with M&M's), you could probably take a point away from me with that little nugget of truth. Most people don't make that choice after high school. When young adults are finally staring down a hope of independence, most of them don't choose to go to a school with more rules than their parents' house. But I did.

We had a curfew of midnight on school nights and 1:00 a.m. on the weekends.

We had chapel at 10:00 every morning, and we had to budget our "skips."

We had a dress code where men had to wear collared shirts and nice pants, and women had to wear skirts.

(They did give us a ten-week respite for winter quarter because . . . cold. And let me tell you, we girls made the most of our khakis and corduroys while freedom rang.)

(And, to be clear, even winter at this school wasn't cold enough for jeans. Freedom only rang so far.)

We had room checks to make sure we had made our beds, emptied our trash, and hung up our knee-length skirts.

When I got a job waitressing at a restaurant in town, I had to get special permission from campus security because official policy allowed no reason for a freshman to have a car on campus.

No dancing allowed.

No card playing.

Only one TV existed in the dorm, where we squeezed together as many women as possible to watch George Clooney on *ER* every Thursday night. (But I assure you, nobody was allowed to watch *Will and Grace*.)

Some experts say college is your last chance to influence a child; others say it's your first chance to influence an adult. It's hard to know where the writers of the code of conduct placed themselves on the spectrum, but they made sure we agreed to it with a fresh signature at the start of every school year. The one thing that made it all okay was that we could list exactly two colleges with rules stricter than ours.

Please hear me well: I'm not sorry I went to school there—it is an accredited school with great rankings, reputation, and elite alumni who are successful and respected. I learned from professors I am still in touch with, I took classes I still think about, and I lived with roommates I still love so much.

I'm just not sure *why* I chose to go there. Except for the fact that I adored my second-grade teacher and literally decided when I was in second grade that I would pattern my career path after hers. When she said that's the college she went to, I made my choice.

I was seven.

It wasn't a bad choice because like I said, it wasn't a bad school. But I often wonder if I would have still chosen it if I had visited even one other college or university. I'm not sure I really thought it through. I made up my mind early on, and I let that be my choice. I loved the story, and I stayed the course. I didn't know what I didn't know, and I made my decision based on the information I allowed myself to have.

It worked out fine for a while—a whole year, in fact. And then, a week before my sophomore year began, a spot opened to become an RA (resident assistant) in my dorm. I jumped at the chance to lead and love the women in my circle, plus I didn't hate the situation called "free room and board." That was not nothing. That tuition boost meant fewer hours serving biscuits and gravy to truck drivers barreling down the interstate. I said yes.

But I didn't realize the one hitch in the plan: My new role came with a notepad for writing demerits to my peers. Suddenly, it was my job to make sure the skirts were long enough, the trash cans were emptied, the sheets were tucked, and the doors were locked at midnight. It was a subtle shift of tectonic magnitude. I didn't like it one bit.

I had been able to obey the rules well enough. After all, I was compliant enough to choose a school with so many rules in the first place. But enforcing them? That was a whole different thing. I realized the difference: The rules did not match my convictions.

I did my job as well as I could. I kept an eye out for spaghetti straps. I issued a Room Check pass to everyone on my floor to use whenever they wanted. "Place it on your door, and I won't open it," I said. ("But I won't take it away either," I whispered. "The state of your room is between you and your roommate.") I honestly hated that any of it had to be my business at all.

I didn't last through my sophomore year. In part, it was the endless score keeping and chip counting and rule keeping. But then I fell in love with Robb (already a college grad and starting a career), and there wasn't a single place on campus where I was allowed to kiss this man who had asked me to marry him.

And that was my undoing.

I transferred at the end of winter quarter. I took my contraband jeans and my college credits, moved back home where I could even choose to wear jeans, and went to the university nearby.

There was a time when the rules had been okay with me. But then I learned that it's a heavy load to carry, finding and keeping track of everything everyone else is doing wrong (or even thinking about doing wrong).

There was a time when I knew all the rules and thought the best people followed them.

I didn't know what I didn't know.

I didn't know I was wrong.

o——o

In the Bible, there are a lot of rules. I find it so interesting to read through the many laws in the book of Leviticus and notice which ones we keep and which ones we don't.

- "Do not insult the deaf or cause the blind to stumble."[52]
- "Keep my Sabbath days of rest, and show reverence toward my sanctuary."[53]
- "Stand up in the presence of the elderly, and show respect for the aged."[54]

Still good rules to live by, right?

But then I come across others—

- "Do not wear clothing woven from two different kinds of thread."[55]
- "Do not trim off the hair on your temples or trim your beards."[56]

I am a fan of a good linen blend and a well-kempt beard. Why do these rules no longer feel like they apply to life and faith?

Those Old Testament people had many rules. The rules were there for a specific reason—because they couldn't keep all of them perfectly. It was an every-moment reminder of how sin had broken their relationship with God, and nothing they could do by themselves could put it back together. So much separation. So much guilt. So much awareness of shame and uncleanliness. So much to do to make it right, even when they didn't know what they had done wrong, when they had sinned unintentionally. Still guilty! And so much work to do to be forgiven! Reading these long lists, I began to feel an inch of understanding of the exhausting demands of holiness.

But even in the midst of the endless rules, I see this theme over and over: *I am the Lord Your God.* God was still there, still their God, even as he waited for them to realize how much they needed him.

After slogging through these hard chapters, I see now why it was such a big deal—and so offensive to so many rulekeepers—for Jesus to arrive on the scene and start offering blankets of forgiveness in exchange for belief. In a playful parallel of my imagination, I hear generational Jews saying to newly converted Gentiles, *"What? It can't be that easy! It has never been that easy! Why, when I was your age, we had to memorize the entire Torah. We had to hunt*

*for our own pigeons to sacrifice at the altar. We couldn't eat pork.
Why, we had to be circumcised, for goodness' sake. Kids these days."*

But Jesus rocked the boat. He raised some questions. He made
them aware of what they didn't know. All because he was preparing
to present a new way of living and offer himself as the sacrifice for
sins—and for all the rules they'd ever broken.

○———○

The first few chapters in the New Testament book of Acts are some
of my favorites, though I find that I say that about more and more
chapters as I study the Bible. But this story of the very beginning
of what we call "the church" is so tender to me. Jesus' followers are
taking their first steps into adulthood, so to speak.

Jesus had lived, died, and lived again.

His followers thought they were right, then wrong, then right
again.

They were trying to decide what to do now, and I imagine they
felt a fair measure of guilt for what they had done: The Pharisees—
the most religious people of their day—had killed Jesus. I imagine
it was probably hard to know how to move forward.

In the second chapter of Acts, a crowd gathers around these
followers of Jesus, and Peter speaks to the crowd: "People, listen.
God knew what would happen. This plan was prearranged, and it
was carried out when Jesus was betrayed. With the help of others,
you nailed him to a cross and killed him. . . . So, let everyone know
for sure that God has made this Jesus—remember, the one *whom
you crucified*—to be both Lord and Messiah!"[57]

And then, in a different conversation, he goes on to say this:
"Friends, I realize that what you and your leaders did to Jesus was
done in ignorance."[58]

Let's just take a minute to sit with that. He's acknowledging that there are mistakes we can make in ignorance. And, honestly, it's kind of an understatement. Is there any greater "mistake" than the people completely missing who Jesus is—and killing him for saying who he is?

I think the people in Jerusalem believed that calling for Jesus' death was righteousness. They thought they were in the right. They believed that, by ridding the world of this man they could not understand, they were defending the integrity of God and the prophesy about the Messiah. They thought they were following all the right rules, while in reality, they just didn't recognize the Messiah when they met him.

They didn't know what they didn't know.

This stops me in my tracks, I have to tell you. It's so easy to see myself in those Pharisees. In those people who thought they were right but were so wrong. There was a time in my legalist history when I would have made that same decision, thinking I was the one on the right side of the law.

There are times when we can think we are right and yet, as it turns out, we are completely wrong. And the Bible says this loud and clear to us:

There is a path before each person that seems right, but it ends in death.[59]

Now we see things imperfectly, like puzzling reflections in a mirror, but then we will see everything with perfect clarity. All that I know now is partial and incomplete, but then I will know everything completely, just as God now knows me completely.[60]

Sometimes we get it wrong even in our efforts to get it right, all because we don't know all there is to know. That's the very nature of ignorance.

As Peter is addressing the men and women in those opening chapters of Acts, he gives the antidote for ignorance:

> *Repent of your sins and turn to God, so that your sins may be wiped away.*
>   *Then times of refreshment will come from the presence of the Lord.*[61]

Now, let's be clear: Ignorance is not a sin. It's not a sin to not know. It's one of the reasons parents always have to be careful not to punish kids for a mistake, only for willful choices to disobey. Because it's not a sin to *not know*.

But what I *do* in my ignorance—my decisions, my actions, my will? I can absolutely make sinful choices that can hurt people, break relationships, damage my influence, and lead to greater sins.

The Bible is important in our actual lives because it brings to light what we've been believing wrongly, thinking wrongly, where we've been acting out of ignorance, thinking we're following God when instead we're just in lockstep with some human's rules based on *their* ignorance about what God really wants.

Sometimes we approach the Bible thinking its purpose is to give us a list of rules to follow, and in our humanness, we then add rules on top of rules on top of rules. A teacher of mine once described this as a series of concentric circles: The bullseye is what God actually said, but then we try to protect ourselves from transgressing in that one thing, so we add a circle of another rule, and then another, and another.

When my dad was teaching me to drive on busy highways,

he explained that generally the best place for me to be is in the middle lane. Leave the right lane open for people who are entering the highway and need room to merge, and leave the left lane open for people who need to get around the traffic. It would have been extreme to decide, in an effort to follow my dad's suggestions, that I should never, ever, under any circumstances, go anywhere near that left lane. And worse, I could have concluded that *nobody* should drive in that left lane, and I could have called the police every time I saw someone tootling down the highway like they owned the place.

Obviously, this feels extreme. But in some ways, isn't it what we do? It's what the Pharisees did: They created a bunch of Extra Rules to prevent people from getting too close to accidentally breaking the Actual Rules.

Our culture and country are checkered with a history in which many people, including a whole lot of Christians, have done truly deplorable, dehumanizing things to one another. Sometimes, the line between ignorance and evil is alarmingly thin. How could these have ever been acceptable? Because of Ignorance. These choices fit with beliefs at the time. Because somebody said it was appropriate, and we believed them.

But now we know better. We can see clearly now, and we would never go back to the way things were, now that we know.

So I can't help but wonder . . . what decisions, laws, and arguments are we battling now because they seem like a good idea? What will obviously be recognized and deemed incorrect later, when we know more? What have we misunderstood about God and the Bible because of Ignorance, but as we come to understand his heart and his Word better, we'll believe better?

We can't know yet. Because of Ignorance. It's an ongoing journey, the growing awareness of decisions we need to correct and actions we need to rectify, now that we know what we didn't know.

There are a lot of issues that divide, and where left and right feel fluid and tricky.

There are issues of justice where the scales are so close to each other that I don't know which way things should tilt.

There are places where the laws are changing, but I'm not sure what God's heart is.

To be honest, there are so many places where *I just plain do not know.*

So what should I do when I don't know what to do? How am I supposed to take a single step in this world of uncertainty?

The writers of the Bible give us these instructions:

- "Do nothing out of selfish ambition or vain conceit."[62]
- "Do everything in love."[63]
- "Be humble, thinking of others as better than yourselves."[64]
- "Keep on loving one another as brothers and sisters."[65]
- "Serve one another."[66]
- "Be at peace with each other."[67]
- "Accept one another."[68]
- "Forgive anyone who offends you."[69]
- "Think of ways to motivate one another to acts of love and good works."[70]

In a word: *Love.*

Throughout the Bible, in different words and different ways, we see it over and over: We are commanded to *love.* There are no exceptions to this, and this rule does not change. Jesus did this again and again.

Love your neighbors by sharing what you have.

Love the people you see in the grocery store.

Love the person who cuts you off in traffic.

Love with every extension of your voice and your interactions, from your Facebook posts to your texting dialogues. (Remember: There is only one you, not the internet you and the in-person you.)

Love with the way your faith interacts with the people around you. Don't use Scripture like a weapon. Yes, it is a sword of truth, but as Anne Lamott says, "You don't always have to chop with a sword of truth. You can point, too."[71]

When you are not sure what to do, where to step, and which rules apply, *choose the most loving act toward the person in front of you.*

When your theology shifts, when you are confused about the minor issues, focus on the major one: *Love the person in front of you.*

⚬——————⚬

Over the most recent decades of my life, I have discovered that I am ignorant in ways I don't even know. And that is some scary stuff to hold in my hands, this sharpening awareness of what seems right but might be wrong. I am sometimes retroactively shocked by my decisions, by this category in life that I call "Things that seemed like a good idea at the time."

Haircuts. Paint colors. People I've dated.

I promise you this: I didn't want to make the wrong choice. Who wants to be wrong? Nobody. Though I try not to willfully do the wrong thing, sometimes I still do the wrong thing. And when I look back on a decision and wonder what on earth I was thinking, I can recognize with grace that I have more information now. Back then, I made the choice that seemed like a good idea at the time.

You know the funny meme that says, "I'm sorry for what I did when I was hungry"? Maybe that's the first step out of ignorance.

- "I'm sorry for what I did. It seemed like a good idea at the time, and now I know it wasn't."
- "I'm sorry for what I said when I didn't know."
- "I'm sorry for what I said in my ignorance."
- "I didn't know what I know now. Please forgive me."

God, be in the spaces of my ignorance. Fill in the gaps of what I don't know that I don't know.

Be Lord over my ignorance. Forgive me for what I did when I didn't know. Refresh me with your presence. Let me lead with love, especially when I do not know what to do.

Which is . . . well, nearly always.

Amen.

Practice for Your Actual Life

There's a famous story in the Bible about Jesus publicly forgiving a woman caught in adultery.[72] Jesus was teaching the crowds when the rulekeepers of religious law stormed up, dragging the woman to him, saying the law required her to be stoned. They kept demanding an answer (and a death sentence), and we can imagine they caused quite a scene. That's how people are when they want someone to take the heat, when they want a public disgrace, when they want to prioritize rules above relationship.

And Jesus says, "All right, but let the one who has never sinned throw the first stone!"[73]

The writer says that when the accusers heard this, they slipped away, one by one, beginning with the oldest (we daresay the wisest), until only Jesus was left in the middle of the crowd with the woman.

"Where are your accusers? Didn't even one of them condemn you?" he asked.

"No, Lord," she said.

And Jesus said, "Neither do I. Go and sin no more."[74]

When we study the choices of Jesus, we can see the behavior he commended and the faithfulness he loves. He was quiet and gentle in his tone. He chose the individual instead of the mob mentality. And he stood with her until they left her alone.

When people take sides and throw stones of criticism at others, look instead at the ones in the line of fire. Show them you love them. Stay with them until the mob quiets, until the loud voices fade away. It doesn't matter if you agree with their choices. Jesus didn't agree with the woman's, but he loved her in a language she understood: Presence.

We have one rule: LOVE. Choose to love the person in your path, no matter what.

No. Matter. What.

We're supposed to just love the people in front of us. . . . We don't need to spend as much time as we do telling people what we think about what they're doing. Loving people doesn't mean we need to control their conduct. There's a big difference between the two. Loving people means caring without an agenda. As soon as we have an agenda, it's not love anymore. It's acting like you care to get someone to do what you want or what you think God wants them to do. Do less of that, and people will see a lot less of you and more of Jesus.

BOB GOFF, *Everybody, Always*

CHAPTER 7

Imagine That Dinner Table

Know the People

My Grams loved to tell a joke about that famous painting of the Last Supper, about Jesus and the disciples arriving at the upper room. In her retelling, John checks in with the maître d', like it's a fine Italian restaurant. When the host asks how many are in their party, John says, "We need seating for twenty-six, please."

But the host looks all quizzical, and he does a quick head count. He says, "But sir, there are only thirteen of you. Will more be joining your party?"

And John replies, "You are right: Twelve disciples and Jesus. But we all have to sit on one side of the table for the photo."

The thing is, there was a real supper. The table would have looked different (back then, it was customary for people to lay on couches as they ate, with their heads near a low table and their feet stretched out behind them), but these were real people, real friends, gathered to share a meal together. The Bible is full of meals and meetings, of people eating grilled fish and bread, figs and pomegranates. It's not hard to picture the food, but sometimes it can be harder to picture the people. Sometimes, we get so caught up in the stories, we forget that these people were real.

If you could sit in on any meal in the Bible, which one would you choose? There are *so many to choose from*.

There's the wedding where Jesus performed the first miracle, when he turned water into wine. Weddings were weeklong festivities, and running out of wine was an embarrassing miscalculation and a breach of the unwritten rules of hospitality. Mary came to Jesus and said, "They have no more wine." To which her son replied, "That's not our problem. My time has not yet come."

But his mother told the servants, "Do whatever he tells you."[75] She knew what he was capable of, and she wanted the party to continue. Sure enough, Jesus had the servants fill six stone jars with water, and he produced an estimated 120 to 180 gallons[76] of wine for the party. If we ever imagine God as dull or boring, then we should consider him in that moment, telling the guests to party on.

I read that story and wonder, *Did Jesus intend to perform his first public miracle that day?* Jesus was sinless, so we know he wasn't annoyed, but how did he feel when his mother intervened and told him what to do? Did he change his mind because Mary asked him? Maybe he was relieved to finally get to stretch his miracle muscles, to finally do what he was capable of doing. If Mary hadn't asked, nobody would have known that the wine came from Jesus that day. And so if that's true, then how many things might he be waiting to do, if only we would ask him? When we ask for big things—bigger than us—we can be sure it is God who answers and provides.

Or how about that time when a Pharisee invited Jesus to have dinner at his home, and when "a certain immoral woman from that city heard he was eating there, she brought a beautiful alabaster jar filled with expensive perfume."[77] She was uninvited, but she entered the house anyway and knelt behind Jesus at his feet as he lounged on the cushions by the table.[78] It's an awkward scene to picture because it's so different from what we do, but then the story takes this beautiful turn. The woman intended to come and pour out her perfume, but suddenly she found herself weeping. I really don't think she planned this emotional display, but sometimes when we meet someone we've longed to meet, our emotions get ahead of us. Her tears were falling on his feet. I imagine her feeling overcome, not knowing what to do, wishing for a towel, and not having a towel, so what does she use to dry his feet? Her hair. And then, with her hair now wet with her tears and this perfume, she's all in. She starts kissing his feet and pouring more perfume on them.

Again, let's admit: It's awkward.

But there's something so unstoppably authentic about her worship in that moment. She wanted to be near Jesus, to give him what she had to give, and then things started spiraling out of control. She may have been tempted to slip away into the night, to hope nobody saw her, but she leaned right into it. The men at the table scoffed and whispered about her, but she didn't care what they saw, what they thought. She just needed to worship Jesus, tears and perfume and wet hair notwithstanding. The woman wouldn't be stopped.

That is worship, that extravagant and obvious overflow of gratitude.

Sometimes I feel like I have to apologize for strong emotions, especially if I'm crying in public or responding in a way that might seem over-the-top to onlookers. But then I think of this woman, who was all in. She wouldn't apologize for her tears, for that would be apologizing for the truth. Her sin was the greatest thing she could imagine, until she encountered Jesus' forgiveness—that outmatched anything she'd ever done. She was overcome and undone, in a public way. Goodness, I can't wait to meet her.

Then there's that really gory dinner, the disturbing story about the death of John the Baptist.[79] John was the miracle baby born to very-very-old, long-past-childbearing-years Elizabeth, who was cousin to the Virgin Mary. The entire purpose of John's life was to draw attention to Jesus. Back then, when significant Roman officials made a public appearance, someone else appeared before them, heralding the way, making sure the people didn't miss the grand entrance.[80] So John's mission was to announce the arrival of the most important man who ever lived. The man was born with a job to do. And he was a wild man, unstoppable, a prophet with determination and a loud voice.

I always thought that John's holy purpose should come with some guarantees for a happy ending to his life, for some special favor and personal miracles. But it didn't go that way. When King Herod married his halfbrother's former wife and John called him out on his immoral behavior, the king and queen didn't love his truth telling. King Herod had John killed as a favor to his new wife, and the Bible says they delivered John's head to her on a platter—*at the king's birthday party*! Do you think they showed it to everyone with a lot of pomp and circumstance? Do you think they paraded that platter all around the room to make sure everyone got a good look at his matted beard, his eyelids open and his gaze empty? What a horrific meal.

But you wouldn't have to pick that one—there are so many

meals to choose from. Think about the beach breakfast in the Gospel of John. In the hours before Jesus was killed, Peter denied three times that he knew him. They had done life together, eaten meals together. This teacher and student were close friends. But when his own life was on the line, Peter severed ties. He said time and time again, "I don't know him."[81]

And then Jesus died. Their friend, mentor, teacher, Savior . . . gone.

The fishermen disciples decided to get back to their work on the boats, because what else could they do? I feel such tenderness when I imagine those men, barely holding it together, the raw grief of those few days after Jesus was gone. There was rumor that the tomb was empty, but that story had seemed like nonsense to these men. John and Peter had even visited the tomb, they saw the grave linens folded up like nobody had worn them, and things were awfully strange and weird and questionable. But they hadn't seen Jesus yet. They didn't know if he was coming back, or if it had all been a mistake. Everything was up in the air, all unknown, yet seemingly finished and over. I imagine they had to wonder if it was all a lie.

And then Jesus came to the shore one morning, alongside where they had been fishing all night. I imagine him calling out to them, "Hey, fellas, are you catching any fish out there?"

"No," they answered him, likely with little interest in this man pestering them with distractions from the shore.

And then I picture Jesus, putting his hands like a megaphone to his mouth, and calling out, "Put your nets on the other side of the boat, and you'll get some!"

So they did, and they couldn't haul in the net because there were so many fish in it. At the sight of this crazy amount of fish, and at the sound of this familiar voice on the shore, John was the one to put two and two together. He recognized Jesus and said to Peter, "It is the Lord!"[82]

And then Peter—the one who had been able to walk on water—jumps right out of the boat and into the sea. He jumps in, wearing his tunic, swimming with his heavy clothes on, because he just can't wait to get to Jesus. He cannot wait one more minute.

Can you imagine his relief? He had to have felt so much guilt, so much shame, like he had let Jesus down by denying him, confirming the very betrayal Jesus had predicted.

And all of his buddies stayed with the boat and pulled the loaded nets in. When they get to the shore to discover that Jesus had put some fish on the grill, and he's made some bread for them—and, I just thought of this—maybe that was a miracle in itself. Bread takes more than a few minutes to whip together, and I am guessing the fish weren't just lying there on the shore, waiting to be cooked. Jesus had produced and prepared this food for them, the most beautiful breakfast in history.

Imagine that moment when Peter got to Jesus. Imagine the embrace between Jesus and Peter, these two dear friends, united again. Imagine the moment when the other disciples realized who he was. He was far enough away that they couldn't see him up close, but they could recognize his voice, and I imagine they knew his silhouette . . . and they just had to get to him. They *had* to.

You're invited into the story, and the story is invited into you. I love this practice for any story. Anything we can do to cut through the layers of boredom that have grown over a story, anything we can do to rediscover the freshness, to resurrect the unpredictability of what happened—this brings us into the story all over again. Put yourself in the story as often as you can.

Imagine these moments:

In the moments before Jesus' arrest, when Judas brought the centurions to the garden in the grove of olive trees. And Jesus stepped forward to say, "Who are you looking for?"

And they said, "Jesus the Nazarene."

And Jesus said, "I Am he."

And the passage says, "They all drew back and fell to the ground!"[83]

I wonder—did they fall to the ground in recognition of who he really was? Or did the Spirit slay them to the ground in surrender? What must that have been like for them, lying on the ground? Did they wonder at what they were about to do?

Or consider how Moses named himself very humble, "more than all the men on the face of the earth,"[84] and how John calls himself "the disciple Jesus loved."[85] When John and Peter raced to the empty tomb, John wrote, "They were both running, but the other disciple outran Peter and reached the tomb first."[86] I love his desire to be first, a man among men. The *best*. I have such tenderness in my heart for men with such insecurities—on record.

Imagine Mary Magdalene outside the empty tomb. She thought Jesus was the gardener,[87] which makes me wonder if I would recognize Jesus if he appeared to me, before me. What would it be like to hear Jesus say your name, just as he called out to Mary?

In Henri Nouwen's book *The Return of the Prodigal Son*, he invites us readers to put ourselves in Jesus' parable as every character: the father who loves his sons so much; then as the younger brother whose arrogance and shame make him believe he has fallen from his dad's love; then as the older brother who thinks he has solidly earned his father's love by keeping all the rules. I love this practice for any story.

Have you ever stopped to think about the fact that the people in the Bible are real people—not footnotes in history or the two-dimensional cardboard cutouts and flannelgraph characters of Sunday school? They're not flawless humans who always get it right. They're ordinary people, with flesh and blood, skin and bone, strengths and weaknesses, favorite foods and favorite colors. People who struggle with insecurity and anxiety and sleepless nights and ugly secrets. People just like us—trying to accept the truth and live within the boundaries that bring freedom, taking risks of all sizes and wondering if they got it right.

Why is it important to see the people of the Bible as real people? When we see the people of the Bible as real people, we begin to understand that their God is our God too. Jesus seemed to be a genuine foodie, and I dearly love this about him. He spent so much of his time eating and drinking, at tables in people's homes and on grassy hillsides. He did life with them, and when we consider their humanity, the struggles, the mistakes—all of this helps us understand that we can be at rest in God as he's growing us and guiding us through our stories because we've already seen how he is with people he loves. When we see that these people were real people, we can see that he is with us—pointing us to who he is in our lives because of who he has revealed himself to be in the Bible.

As a bonus, we can let these real people of the Bible become real teachers in our lives. Mentors are the people we look toward to educate and inspire us, to know what we should do—or not do. When we let ourselves into the story, as we picture ourselves in the crowd or imagine what it was like to be one of Jesus' disciples, we can make these people mentors in our actual lives.

- Learn from Noah how to start with the instructions you have and get busy right now, even if there's not yet a cloud in the sky. (Genesis 6–9)
- Let Hannah teach you to pray through sorrow and to keep the promises you make. (1 Samuel 1)
- Let Cain show you that nobody is immune to making a terrible choice and uncontrolled anger will always lead to regret. (Genesis 4)
- Let Sarah teach you that we can't guess how God will work in our lives, that his plans play out in ways we may never fully understand. (Genesis 18)
- Let David show you that all sin can be forgiven, but that God doesn't always deliver us from consequences. (2 Samuel 11–12; Psalm 32)
- Learn from John the Baptist that sometimes you need to step aside for someone who is more gifted than you. (Matthew 3:11-12)
- Learn from Samson that giftedness is not the same as godliness, that all the tools to do the right things can be erased by pride, stubbornness, and selfish passion. (Judges 16:1-22)
- Let Moses and Joshua show you how mentoring makes a good person even better. (Exodus 24)
- Learn from Joseph that it's not a good idea to brag about yourself, lest your brothers fake your death and toss you into a well. (Genesis 37) (I'm smiling as I type this, because obviously Joseph's fascinating life story has *far more to teach us* than that. Which is the whole point.)

Read for yourself. Put yourself there. Respond to Jesus' words of love and encouragement. And remember that Jesus came for us who live today, as well as those who lived two thousand years ago.

He was to them what he is to us, a God who is faithful, kind, unchanging, and unfailing. When we explore the stories of the past with intention and imagination, then we can engage the God of our present moment.

Practice for Your Actual Life

Lectio Divina means *divine reading* or *sacred reading*, and it is an ancient practice of using our senses to interact with the text. You can do this with any sacred text, and I'm especially fond of the parables and psalms. The method includes four phases:

- Reading
- Reflecting
- Responding
- Resting

Here's what it looks like.

First, be still. Take a few deep breaths.

In Phileena Heuertz's book *Mindful Silence*, I learned about the practice of Breath Prayer. It is "an ancient Christian prayer practice dating back to at least the sixth century," and it's also "known as the Jesus Prayer or Prayer of the Heart."[88]

Our natural breath pattern aligns easily with a phrase or a short sentence that is six to eight syllables. Breath prayer is choosing a praise or petition, a thank-you or an ask, and aligning it with your inhale and exhale.

I like to do the Breath Prayer here to begin. *Holy Spirit, show me.*

During Reading, use your senses and your imagination as you read the text you've chosen. Sometimes it's interesting to read it out loud to yourself, to listen to the words instead of just observing them silently. You'll catch things differently, and you might feel like you're in the scene, especially those dramatized in the Gospels or the books that started out as letters to a group of people. Take in all the sights, sounds, textures, and even smells of the scene. Imagine as deeply and as far as you can.

During Reflecting, listen for a word or phrase that gets your attention. Watch for something to jump out at you. Consider why it may have grabbed you. With great reverence, carefully observe what God has said. Picture it. Meditate on it. Take time to absorb the truth in the words, to think about how they can instruct you, encourage you, and give you wisdom and hope.

In Responding, read the text a third time, and tell God your response. Turn what you have learned into a prayer. Ask him your questions. Be still and listen for answers. Wait for clarity. Tell him your heart's response.

During Resting, read one final time, and then rest in your experience. Give your new understanding some room to breathe and a space to live within you.

Take these my small offerings:
 my pen, my paper, my words, my willingness
 to be still and present.

Fill my imagination.
 Be to me both fire and wonder,
 Inspiration and guide.

DOUGLAS MCKELVEY, *Every Moment Holy*

CHAPTER 8

Even If He Doesn't

When God Says No

MY HUSBAND PETER AND I have two very different stories of faith miracles.

He begged and pleaded with God from a desperate place in a jail cell, and God told him yes. The miracle is that he was set free.

I begged and pleaded with God from a desperate place on my bedroom floor, and God told me no. The miracle is that my faith stayed intact at all.

When we pray together, when we ask God for things, it sounds different. Peter prays for miracles in the hope of a heart-stretching yes; I pray for comfort in the likelihood of a heartbreaking no.

Peter said one day, "Tricia, God could say yes."

"Yes, but sometimes he says no."

"It says in Matthew, if you have faith the size of a mustard seed, you can toss this mountain into the sea."[89]

"Then why did God let Robb die? Does that mean I didn't have enough faith?"

It had started as a simpler conversation, but I was suddenly crying, and undoubtedly Peter felt like he was in over his head. This conversation had taken a difficult turn. In my experience, most conversations like this don't tie themselves up with a tidy bow. They tie in knots of difficult tension.

I don't like a theology of healing that says it all depends on my faith. Because what does that mean when God doesn't say yes? Does it mean I didn't have enough faith? And is a lack of faith my fault?

If faithfulness is a fruit of the Holy Spirit, then is it his job to grow it in me? If I don't have it, then how in the world do I get it? And is it my fault that someone is sick—or dying—because of my "lack of faith?"

That really doesn't feel good. I don't like that at all.

○———○

As I've looked to fall in love with God's words in my actual life, I have encountered lots of the times when he said yes to people. If you have experienced a time when Jesus said yes, you may feel drawn to the stories where he said yes to other people too. But if he has told you no, then maybe those stories aren't your favorite.

Like this one, the story of the woman who followed Jesus through the crowd, knowing that if she could just touch his robe, she would be healed.

Just then a woman who had been subject to bleeding for twelve
years came up behind him and touched the edge of his cloak.
She said to herself, "If I only touch his cloak, I will be healed."

Jesus turned and saw her. "Take heart, daughter," he said, "your faith has healed you." And the woman was healed at that moment.[90]

That story used to really make me mad. I even said from a stage once, "Does the Word of God ever make you furious?"

(I actually said something worse than that, but it's how I felt. I was angry then. And fairly loose with my word choices.)

I hear my therapist in my head, reminding me that I may have clarity now that I didn't have then, so I don't have to look down on the person I was and the perspective I had with my limited knowledge. I can look with compassion on where I was, how I felt, and how it led me to where I am now. I felt angry then, but I get it now. Robb has been gone for nearly a decade, and in that long stretch of time, I have in fact healed. The wound of his death is a scar that lives in the landscape of my life, not a bleeding wound that covers everything anymore. I have healed.

And how did I find that healing? Where did that healing come from?

It came from faithfulness to trust the God who could have healed Robb. The healing came in staying with the path, as Eugene Peterson says, from long obedience in the same direction.[91] It came from being honest with the Lord, with my family, and with myself, about how I felt and what I was wondering about, hurting over, healing from. The healing came in my willingness to stay the course. To be faithful to the journey.

When I read the story of Jesus healing the woman who was bleeding, I imagine others probably felt jealous of her that day, jealous of her healing. Others likely touched his robe. The magic wasn't in touching his robe—it was in her belief that he could heal her. It was in her faithfulness to chase after him. And honestly, imagining those other people in the crowd, I can see now what fueled my distrust of that verse and that story. I, too, was jealous of her and her healing.

We want Jesus to work in the ways we expect him to, in a way that makes logical, mathematical sense. Like in Jesus' parable of the vineyard workers, he tells a story of those who believed their reward was due to them because they had served longer, worked harder, been more faithful. But it's God's choice to do what he wants with the power and sovereignty that he has.[92] Healing is not neat and easy in the Bible either, and the stories in those pages give us a glimpse of miracles, yes, but also of people who didn't get the miracle. The Bible helps us understand that God is more complicated than we'd like, and healing is too.

I've looked also at the story of Lazarus, of the day he was dying and how his two sisters sent word to Jesus: "Lord, your dear friend is very sick."[93] The sisters probably weren't frantic yet, at least in my imagination. They were worried but thankful that they knew the man who could fix it. And they didn't just know him in the way that everybody knew him; he was a friend of theirs. He was a friend close enough that he had been a guest and eaten a meal in their home.[94] He was more than a passing acquaintance. He was their dear friend. He could fix this.

When Jesus got their message, he said, "Lazarus's sickness will not end in death. No, it happened for the glory of God so that the Son of God will receive glory from this."[95]

He gave them hope. *This will all be okay,* they likely thought. But then he didn't come right away. Faith can be this kind of roller coaster of encouragement and discouragement, when I think God's words mean one thing, and then I learn that they mean something else. Or when I read a verse that says, "If you make the LORD . . . your shelter, no evil will conquer you; no plague will come near your house,"[96] and when there's no plague going on, it's comforting, sure. But I'm reluctant to tell my children these words in the face of the pandemic currently raging around the world, when literally tens of thousands are dying around us. I am afraid to give them this formula to cling to . . . because what if we get sick? That is the moment when they will most need their faith, and I don't want to have given them the very key to question it.

(Why do I feel like I must protect God's reputation? I guess that's how I am with the ones I love. It's like I think, *Sure, I'll keep that little exception to myself. Let's keep you sparkly and shiny and trustworthy. You might not come through the way we're hoping, but let's keep that shadow of you quiet.*)

So the sisters got a dose of encouragement here, but I feel bad for them because Jesus didn't mean what they thought he meant. The verse says, "Although Jesus loved Martha, Mary, and Lazarus, he stayed where he was for the next two days."[97] (A small nugget tucked in here: He didn't come quickly for his close friends. So when he doesn't answer me right away, it doesn't mean he doesn't love me.)

But by the time Jesus arrived on the scene, Lazarus had been in his grave for four days! That's a long time. Long enough for reality to set in. Many had come to console Mary and Martha in their loss. I know what that looks like and feels like, to be physically surrounded by people who love you so much that they had to come, absolutely had to be near you.

Mary and Martha responded differently when they each saw Jesus, which makes sense; we each grieve differently. Raw grief strips you of filters.

Martha said to Jesus, "Lord, if only you had been here, my brother would not have died. But even now I know that God will give you whatever you ask."[98]

Mary's response was a little different. "Lord, if only you had been here, my brother would not have died."[99] Their words match.

I imagine they had been saying these words for days. Maybe it was the only thing they could bring themselves to say. You say only what you can, only what you must, only what is true. There is no space for anything else. I imagine the sisters saying these words with every range of emotion: with longing, in lament, in deep grief, and possibly through the gritted teeth of resentment. *If only he had been here.*

"When Jesus saw her weeping and saw the other people wailing with her, a deep anger welled up within him . . . then Jesus wept."[100]

Stevie Swift has written a most compelling description of this, and her words have stayed with me: "He cried. He knew Lazarus was dead before he got the news. But still, He cried. He knew Lazarus would be alive again in moments. But still, He cried. He knew this world is not our home. He knew death here is not forever. He knew eternity and the Kingdom better than anyone else could. And He wept. Because this world is full of pain and regret and loss and depression and devastation. He wept because knowing the end of the story doesn't mean you can't cry at the sad parts."[101]

Lazarus came back from the dead that day, and Jesus gave all of them their miracle. But that didn't spare any of them from one whiplash of a roller coaster of emotions, wondering what he would do. Believing he could, wondering if he would.

How do we learn to hold both sides of that equation, the belief that God can, but the understanding that he might not? It's the greatest tension of all. The Bible doesn't give us an answer for the tension, but it helps us sit in it. It shows us the heart of God, the deep love and grief and profound power, the mystery of how he thinks and acts and is. The Bible doesn't give us a reason for suffering. It gives us a God who is over it and with us in it, even as we live in the ache.

A trio named Shadrach, Meshach, and Abednego, all the way back in the Old Testament, show us how to hold the tension with both hands. Their friend Daniel is best known for his time in a lion's den, and these pals of his are known for making a stand in a fiery furnace. Both these Bible stories got some airtime in Sunday school, in large part because Daniel and his friends were young men who demonstrated that there is more to being young than making mistakes. Adults are quickly won over by young people who show wisdom and discernment, and Daniel's friends— Shadrach, Meshach, and Abednego—show us the power of their convictions. Together they silently defied King Nebuchadnezzar's order to fall down and worship his gold statue, a tower that was taller than the White House.[102] They chose God, even in the face of certain death.

(King Nebuchadnezzar was a bad guy, yet even he can mentor us: If you find yourself flying into a rage when people don't follow your directions, ask yourself if perhaps your ego is bigger than your authority.)

The king gives these guys "one more chance" to bow down to this statue, "but if you refuse, you will be thrown immediately into the blazing furnace. And then what god will be able to rescue you from my power?"[103]

But the three friends hold their ground. They will not bend their convictions.

Shadrach, Meshach, and Abednego reply, "O Nebuchadnezzar, we do not need to defend ourselves before you. If we are thrown into the blazing furnace, the God whom we serve is able to save us. He will rescue us from your power, Your Majesty. **But even if**

he doesn't, we want to make it clear to you, Your Majesty, that we will never serve your gods or worship the gold statue you have set up."[104]

But even if he doesn't.

They knew what they had asked God to do, and they believed he absolutely could do it. They even said he *would.* And then they finish the sentence with the giant caveat: But even if he doesn't, we will not bow to any other god.

That's the balance right there, resting in the tension between the first sentence and the last, between the left hand and the right.

When we know what we want him to do, we believe he can, and we might even say that he will. And we choose this day to remain faithful to this God.[105] Even if he doesn't.

God is still faithful, even if he doesn't come through the way we want him to.

Listen, I believe God can do anything. That is a complete sentence, with nothing added.

I believe he can perform healing miracles. I just haven't seen it in my life. I believe he can, but I cannot say that he always does because you and I both know that sometimes he doesn't. (Otherwise, probably every person any of us have ever loved would still be alive.)

When you tell me I need to have enough faith in order for God to bring healing, then I feel like you're telling me I must have pure faith without any doubt. I have to put all my faith in my left hand and hold it open to receive the gifts God's waiting to give me, and I should put all my doubt in the right hand, lock it up tight, and throw away the key, just to be sure there's no whisper of question.

But I'm looking at those same two hands, and I see different choices. In one hand is faith: I believe he can do anything. In the other hand is sovereignty. Even if he doesn't, I believe he is still good.

Practice for Your Actual Life

You are allowed—actually welcomed and invited—to "present your requests to God."[106] Tell God exactly what you want him to do. Be explicit. Be bold. Write it down.

And then, follow the example of Shadrach, Meshach, and Abednego, and make the boldest statement yet:

> *But even if you don't do this for me, I will believe you are good. I will believe you are in this. I will believe you are God.*

And if you can't say those words yet with an ounce of conviction, then know you're not alone. The writers of the Bible give us examples of people who needed a step before that one, words to bridge the gap.

- "Make me want to obey!"[107]
- "Help me overcome my unbelief!"[108]

So, if you can't say the words "even if he doesn't," then try these words I have claimed more than once:

- "Jesus, help me to be willing to say those words. Make me willing to be willing."

This truth is behind the words of James 1:6-8, that when you pray "you must believe and not doubt. . . ." This throws many readers into great anxiety, because it looks on the surface as if James is saying we must have absolute psychological certainty in our minds as we petition God. That is not what he is talking about. . . . It means not that you are perfect, or morally pure, or devoid of any uncertainty. It means you have made a decision that God is your God and you are going to ditch all competing concerns the moment you can discern them.

TIMOTHY KELLER, *Prayer*

CHAPTER 9

In the Margins
of Your Actual Days

For When You Have No Time

IT'S POSSIBLE you're reading this and thinking, *Right. All of this sounds well and good, but I have no time. Zero time. Anyone who would write a book like this has no understanding of the narrow margins of my life.*

Maybe you are in college or grad school, navigating the complicated labyrinth of paying to be a professional learner, and you can't recall a time when you read a book for pleasure.

Maybe you're in the workforce, climbing a ladder with countless rungs and glass ceilings and endlessly impossible demands on your time.

Maybe you're in the workforce *and* you're a parent, and you're stretched so thin that your work has become less than exemplary at both the office and home.

Maybe you're sandwiched between caring for teenagers and

aging parents, and every moment that once was yours is now allocated to appointments, conversations, and decisions about people whose livelihood and very happiness depend on you doing the right thing.

I see you.

I cannot speak to every harried season of life, and maybe I haven't yet been on the path you're on today. But I can speak to the time that was (thus far) the most trying for me. And perhaps the strategies of this marginless life might resonate with your busy days.

Let's talk for just a moment to the parents of little people, the moms and dads treading water through the seemingly endless days of the first five years. As my friend Catherine writes, these are the warriors in the trenches of "long days of small things."[109]

When a couple is expecting a new baby, sometimes they toss out requests to other parents for recommendations for what they really should have, must get, truly need. Sometimes a gift registry is in order, for everything from the practical to the purely decorative. You could list things for days, from swings to travel systems to burp cloths to bath cushions to nipple brushes. (These are for use on the bottles, not on the moms.)

I concur. All of these things are great, even if they're not entirely necessary. But can I tell you what I recommend to new parents-to-be?

More underwear. Not for the baby—for the parents.

Seriously, every time you go to Target or Walmart, every time you have a few extra bucks in your pocket, toss another pair in the cart. From the time you see two stripes on the pregnancy test, stock up.

Here's why: Your time is about to not be your own.

This baby will light up your world with eye contact and smiles and hiccups and the magic of baby fingernails—so tiny and yet whole. And so much of your daily routine will be on hold while you learn the axis and orbit of this new sunshine of your life.

A wonderfully normal part of the mind-bending experience of becoming a parent is this: You learn that so very many things can wait, either until tomorrow or until the next life stage.

Except when you personally run out of underwear.

Urgency can escalate and depression can plummet quickly when you have no clean underwear. You can get through another day with dry shampoo and yesterday's T-shirt and yoga pants. But the underwear. Sometimes that situation will not wait. Stock up now.

There are so many things that can get set aside, paused, put on the back burner, and put on hold during those days, weeks, months, and years in the trenches of the tyranny of toddlers. And the Bible was one of the things that got set aside for me.

It's very hard (indescribably difficult) to find time to read the Bible when they're hungry again, when everyone's waiting for Mommy to make dinner, and when you remember *you're* the mom and they're waiting for *you*. When you write *Brush Teeth* and *Comb Hair* on your own to-do list for three reasons: because these are tasks that will stay finished for a few hours (thereby proving that you can accomplish *something* that stays done); because it's a legitimate form of self-care; and because otherwise you'll forget your own basic hygiene tasks in the guiding of others through theirs. I dearly love the role of being a mom; I don't always love the tasks of being a mom. As my friend Bekah DiFelice said, "It is okay to feel smothered by a life that you love, a life you have chosen."[110]

Catherine McNiel wrote, "No one tries to exclude mothers from the 'spiritual life,' but it happens regardless. I hear laments rising up in the hearts of mothers, mourning the losses that this season of nurturing unexpectedly brings: the impossibility of pursuing something soul-creative, something life-giving. *There's no time, space, energy, or money. We'll have to wait until the children are older. Right now I just can't.*[111]

This. This is exactly how I felt, waking to wet diapers and washing high-chair trays and reading bedtime stories ad nauseam and singing loudly in the car so that nobody fell asleep before we could get home for full naps: the golden hour of my day. When I finally had an hour to myself, well, I should confess: The Bible wasn't my go-to book of choice. Sometimes my own nap was what my body—and soul—needed most. I just couldn't give one more moment to someone else, even to the God who made these babies who, though they exhausted me to my very bones, I adored with my whole heart.

In this season of my life, I discovered a miraculous invention: 3 × 5 cards.

Beth Moore muses that God created them on the eighth day.[112] And Anne Lamott often carries one in her back pocket to capture the fleeting thoughts that she wants to write into a book, just in case she doesn't have a notebook on her person.[113] Which is kind of the very definition of parenting: Can someone make *something* easier, just in case I can't carry one more thing?

Here's where we can fall in love with the Bible in our *actual lives*. One verse at a time, on those blessed cards. (Please read *blessed* with two syllables here. Bless-ed. It's important to me that you hear it the way I'm saying it, and these cards are a two-syllable blessing.)

In rare moments I was alone—and I do mean rare, and I don't really mean *alone*—I would write a meaningful verse down on a card and slide it into my pocket.

Now, let's talk about the definition of "meaningful verse." Let's agree that all the words of the Bible are holy and good, all valuable and important, all worthy of their own 3 × 5 cards. But they don't all make equal sense, and they're not all easy to wrap your mind around when you have seventeen seconds to yourself before somebody opens the bathroom door because he wants to watch you go potty. Pick some good ones, easy and basic truths, that you can read and absorb on the fly.

Here are some of my favorites:

Salvation is found in no one else, for there is no other name under heaven given to mankind by which we must be saved. Acts 4:12

You will seek me and find me when you seek me with all your heart. Jeremiah 29:13

I am trusting you, O LORD,
   saying, "You are my God!"
My future is in your hands. . . .
Let your favor shine on your servant. Psalm 31:14-16, NLT

You came near when I called you,
   and you said, "Do not fear." Lamentations 3:57

Or this one, especially helpful on long days:

We also pray that you will be strengthened with all his glorious power so you will have all the endurance and patience you need. Colossians 1:11, NLT

Do you see how every single one of those stands on its own? Yes, you can dive into the chapter and book of each verse, and yes, it's good and valuable to know the larger context of God's words—but also, you can worship the Lord at a stoplight by reading this card that's in your cupholder. When I discovered I could read these words in fleeting moments, they began to absorb into my spirit.

I took great heart in the verses in the book of Psalms where the psalmist reminded me that the Lord looks after those who look after the young. God understands the heart—and the demands—of parents in the trenches. And he provides nuggets of daily bread in the form of wisdom in the moment, stoplights to catch your breath, and Goldfish crackers to keep the hunger contained. There is comfort and courage for the tired parents who deeply and desperately love their little ones and simultaneously feel lost beneath the tasks of parenting. Remember, it is okay to feel like you're drowning in a life you created.

When you can't carry the whole Bible with you, when you can't find even one whole minute, you can cut out for yourself a small bite of the whole pie. You can give yourself a nugget of truth that helps lift your eyes above the mess—literally and figuratively. When we stay grounded in the moments that want to sweep us away, God rescues us from putting our identity in something as fickle as good parenting. Even just a few moments with truth can help us orient our perspective to who we are in him.

○———○

I spent years gathering these note cards, carrying them in my pocket, carrying a tattered Ziploc in the diaper bag, keeping the words close. And in a way I couldn't have expected, they met me in my darkest hour.

On the morning that Robb got so sick, so fast, as the paramedics deposited me at the kitchen table so they could work hard to save his life, I reached into my purse and gathered my Scripture cards, the handwritten 3 × 5 companions I'd carried along with me for more than two years. And I will tell you, here and now, in that moment of panic, the Lord quieted my heart with a peace that passes understanding.

I held this card in my hands:

I lift my eyes toward the mountains.
Where will my help come from?
My help comes from the LORD,
the Maker of heaven and earth.

He will not allow your foot to slip;
your Protector will not slumber.
Indeed, the Protector of Israel
does not slumber or sleep.

The LORD protects you;
the LORD is a shelter right by your side.
The sun will not strike you by day
or the moon by night.

The LORD will protect you from all harm;
He will protect your life.
The LORD will protect your coming and going
both now and forever. Psalm 121, HCSB

Again and again, I read those words. Long moments passed. So many. I heard the sounds of rescue upstairs. The sounds of great efforts. The sounds of courageous men doing all they could do.

An officer came into the kitchen. He said quietly, "Are you his wife?"

"I am."

He said, "Ma'am, we've been working on him for forty minutes, and we're doing all we can. But there is no heartbeat or breath sounds, and there have not been any. We're going to need to tell you he has passed."

We're going to need to tell you. As in, not yet, but soon we'll need to. I have since learned that they say it this way to ease the news. Just in case I may fall to the floor and they would have a second patient on their hands, they wanted to break it gently. *We're going to need to tell you.*

My wise and brave mom looked to him and said, "Is that the final word? Is he gone?"

The officer looked to me. "Yes, Ma'am. I'm so very sorry. He's gone."

Have you ever wondered what you might say if a police officer tells you the person you love most has died? I never imagined it this way, but I simply said, "Okay."

And I looked at the tattered card in my hands. On a far brighter day, my own handwriting had captured this truth, now delivering it freshly to me in that moment of shattering awareness.

I lift my eyes toward the mountains.
Where will my help come from?
My help comes from the LORD,
the Maker of heaven and earth.

He is gone. Okay. My help comes from the Lord.

Practice for Your Actual Life

Get yourself to the dollar store, stat. These required ingredients are inexpensive, readily available, and so freeing. Get a stack of 3 × 5 cards, find a sandwich baggie from the drawer, and start your collection of truths to carry in your pocket, glove compartment, or diaper bag.

(Extra points if there are crumbs from Goldfish crackers in the bottom of your Ziploc baggie. Truths with food stains on them are still truth. Sometimes even more tested and trusted.)

Here are some verses to begin your collection:

I have set the LORD always before me.
Because he is at my right hand, I will not be shaken.
Psalm 16:8, EHV

For I am the LORD your God
who takes hold of your right hand
and says to you, Do not fear;
I will help you. Isaiah 41:13

For the word of the LORD holds true,
and we can trust everything he does. Psalm 33:4, NLT

Love one another deeply, from the heart. 1 Peter 1:22

With you there is forgiveness. Psalm 130:4

We will not compare ourselves with each other as if one of us
were better and another worse. We have far more interesting
things to do with our lives. Each of us is an original.
Galatians 5:25-26, MSG

Set a guard over my mouth, LORD;
keep watch over the door of my lips. Psalm 141:3

Though we mamas may appear half crazed, sleep-deprived, harried, and unkempt, our souls are being taught and sharpened and purified. I'm sure of it. We're not able to sit and ponder this, or even be aware of it most of the time. But soul refining is the work of struggle, sacrifice, discomfort, and perseverance.

CATHERINE McNIEL, *Long Days of Small Things*

CHAPTER 10

Fear

The Inhale and Exhale of Truth

A FRIEND ONCE ASKED ME, "Tricia, how can I stop living in fear? I'm worried that something will happen to the person I love, or to my family, or to me. How can I keep that fear from paralyzing me?" These questions—they're so pure, honest, true, and real. *How can I keep from being afraid all the time?*

Max Lucado once told a wonderful story about preparing to travel with his family and holding onto all of their boarding passes until the right time.[114] With a grateful nod to the great Max Lucado, here's what I said to my friend who trusted me to address their greatest fears:

Let's talk about it this way. If you were going on a trip to Mexico next month, you wouldn't carry around your airplane boarding passes this week, right?

You wouldn't, because you don't need them yet. It's not time. And you have other things you need to do with your hands in the meantime, so carrying around those boarding passes would be distracting. It would keep you from doing what you need to do right now, like sending emails and making lunches and loving people and living your life today.

You'd be like, "I sure wish I could set these down. I don't need them yet."

When you worry about what you can't control, about what may—or may not—be waiting around the corner, you are trying to carry things you don't need yet. You tie your hands, and you occupy your thoughts with things you don't have to carry. You do not have to fear the Worst Thing. Here's what I know to be true, because it happened to me.

In the moment of the Worst Thing, it is as if the Spirit places himself in front of you, directly in your line of vision. And he says, "I know you weren't expecting this change of plans, but I knew. I have gone before you and paved the way, and I have everything you need. Here is your boarding pass for the next leg of the trip. I love you, and I'm with you. I'll go with you if you invite me along."

And then he holds out his open hand; he equips you with what you need. Just in time.

When a crisis hits, God hands you a boarding pass. It's called Grace. He'll give it to you when you need it, and not a moment before it's time. You don't need to hold it yet.

Keep your mind—and your hands—free for today. It's the only thing you have to hold.

○———○

Please, let me take a moment here to speak directly to the reader who may have clinical anxiety, just in case this sounds like I am telling you to simply open your hands and release it. Listen: I know it's bigger than that, harder than that, and anyone who says it isn't . . . well, they simply do not know what it is like. I never knew anxiety before Robb died, but it swiftly moved into my life like a bossy, neurotic, terrorist dictator of a roommate. A trip to the mailbox seemed out of control. A day alone with my children presented too many variables, too many unknowns. A grocery list felt like too much information; entering the grocery store felt like sinking into the deep end of the ocean. Maybe you know this kind of anxiety, and it may have come to stay for more than a season in your life. If you're reading this and nodding your head, I feel you. I get you.

So I'm not going to tell you that this can fix it or even minimize it. But I'd like to give you a strategy to ride the wave. Panic is a sweeping current, and if you don't have a plan in place before it crashes over you, you can feel like it's carrying you away with the tide.

Anxiety is a good liar. She had me in her grips for a long time. She makes you believe that you aren't brave, that you cannot handle the next thing, and how you feel now is how you will always feel. The only thing that defeats her is the truth.

The Bible is clear about fear and worry; we aren't supposed to give in to those emotions. I know that, you know that, and it's not news to either of us. But if someone says, "The Bible says not to feel this" to a person who is afraid, that is similar to saying, "You need to calm down" to someone who is flying into a rage. It's . . . not effective. In my own moments of fear and worry, while I understood the value of verses that spoke against them, it was also not necessarily helpful to simply recall verses that told me not to feel what I was currently feeling. Sometimes the only way to stop the repetitive cycle is to interrupt the thoughts themselves. But how?

We may not be able to rid ourselves of it completely, but we can do things that help us to take away some of fear's control over us. If the best way to break a habit is to replace it with another one, then maybe the best thing we can do is put something in our empty hands.

Remember those Scripture cards I told you about in the last chapter? Now's a time to pull those puppies out and put them to work like sled dogs. Meditating on the Word of God offers us time to calm our thoughts, mind, and breathing, even in the face of panic and anxiety. We can "be still, and know,"[115] and the Word of God can quiet the raging storm within.

I found it helpful to call to mind Scripture and promises about who God says he is. He is my rock, my strong fortress, he is close to the brokenhearted and near to those who are crushed in spirit. He is with me in this moment.[116] There is power in the name of Jesus,[117] and to call on Scripture with his very name is to pull on the threads of the tangled mess of my mind.

This is the gift of the Psalms. It's a whole book of honesty and comfort and raw truth. We choose to think the thoughts of God, rather than thoughts that are influenced by fear. When we take our thoughts captive,[118] we make them obedient to Christ. And we have enough for this moment; *this moment* is the only one we're ever in.

○———○

When the Israelites traveled through the wilderness after God rescued them from slavery in Egypt, they began to worry about the scarcity of food. God saw their need, and he provided quail and a kind of bread called manna for them.

Their leader, Moses, told them, "It is the food the LORD has given you to eat. These are the LORD's instructions: Each household should gather as much as it needs. Pick up two quarts for each person in your tent."[119]

This is my favorite part of the story:

The LORD said to Moses, ". . . Each day the people can go out and pick up as much food as they need for that day."[120]

So the people of Israel did as they were told. Some gathered a lot, some only a little. But when they measured it out, everyone had just enough. Those who gathered a lot had nothing left over, and those who gathered only a little had enough. Each family had just what it needed.[121]

He gives us enough for this moment, enough for this day. And then he gives the gift of night, an end to the day, the blessing of starting over with a clean slate. He knew we cannot continue in an endless and ongoing pursuit of anything. But when we take a break, we can start anew, until the next break. We can ask for strength for today. Just today. Always today. God is enough, day by day.

Life is made of days, and days are made of moments. The insurmountable concept of a faithful life can be accomplished in each of us, quietly, day by day, moment by moment, even in the face of fear. Faithfulness in the little things add up to a big life of Faith, because God has given us the ability to decide what our days will be about: We can choose to move toward trust and freedom, one moment at a time.

Psalm 116:10 says, "I believed in you, so I said, 'I am deeply troubled, LORD'" (NLT). I find great comfort in this because one does not cancel out the other. Believing in God does not mean I am not troubled. It means I have a place and a space to say so without spinning my wheels with worry. It means I can tell him—I can be honest about how I am feeling.

I don't have to get my act together *because I believe*. Quite the contrary: I can be honest about my fear *because I believe*.

So how can we conquer fear? By being present in *this day*.

How can we escape anxiety? By being present in *this moment*.

Practice for Your Actual Life

This practice calls for deep, slow breaths. Shallow breaths are often associated with increased feelings of anxiety. In fact, shortness of breath, or hyperventilation, is one of the most common symptoms of panic attacks. Taking fuller breaths allows you feel calmer and in control when faced with panic and anxiety. God gave you your lungs: Use them to their capacity.

On the inhale, you can praise God by calling on his name: Jesus, God, Spirit, Yahweh, Provider, Sustainer, Father, or any other name of adoration.

On the exhale, breathe out your request or praise. Repeat your prayer over and over to the rhythm of your natural breath. Keep your attention on the words of the prayer. If your focus drifts away, as mine always does, gently bring your attention back to your breath and your words—your prayer.

Choose the name you are most comfortable using to invite and invoke the presence of God. Combine it with your request or your praise. Call his name, and tell him what you need. Use your Scripture cards to guide your thoughts, your prayer, and your breath.

Jesus, help me.[122]
Spirit, guide me.[123]
God, heal me.[124]
Wisdom, teach me.[125]
Provider, fix this.
Spirit, be near.
Lord, hear me.[126]
Father, I need you.[127]
God, thank you.[128]
Thank you.[129]
Thank you.[130]
Thank you.[131]
Thank you.[132]

As we deepen our awareness, we are praying all the time . . . Contemplative prayer, like mindfulness, awakens us to listen to what's going on within our body, heart, and mind, and to offer those observations back to God.

PHILEENA HEUERTZ, *Mindful Silence*

CHAPTER 11

Worship

Living Out of the Overflow

DID YOU KNOW THAT *work* is not a four-letter word? There's a misconception about the story of Adam and Eve, that God punished them with having to work as a consequence for their sin, but that's not true. Adam and Eve worked from the day they were created, in the joy and perfection of God's world. God did not give them work to do because they took a bite of the apple,[133] because they broke the one rule. He gave them work to do not because he needed their help. No—he wanted them to see the joy of purpose. The delight of doing what you are made to do.

That felt like a game changer for me, this consideration that the satisfaction I feel from a job well done may not actually be arrogance in my own work but the glittering, sparkling effervescence of God's pleasure in my purpose.

Delight.

My dog is made to chase a squirrel and a tennis ball, to wag his tail when he sees someone he loves. A bird is made to fly and sing. Leaves are made to change color in autumn; the sun is made to rise and shine and own the day; lightning bugs are made to twinkle in the summer evening sky. When creatures do what they are made to do, their existence reflects God's creativity, and their lives are worship to their Maker. When we do what we are made to do, it is worship, connecting with God and celebrating who he is.

Now, let's not get too caught up here in the great questions of vocation, calling, and identifying your purpose and path. What I'm talking about here is anything we do that is creative, caring, and loving. These are the priorities of God, and these reflect his spirit in you and in me. These are worship. God wants our lives to be a celebration of him and the work he has done in us.

Everything is worship throughout the day. When we learn to love the Bible in our actual lives, we find countless kinds of worship present in the pages, worship using all of the senses. When God told his people how to create a meeting place for them and him in the Old Testament, he helped them craft something full of color and beauty and symbolism, and the people worshiped the Lord with what they saw before them. They used their sense of smell by burning incense, a familiar aroma that helped draw their memory and attention to worship.

They utilized their sense of touch in worship, touching the head of the animal to be sacrificed, recognizing the fact that it was taking their place. And—my favorite—they used their sense of taste with intentional foods at the festivals and celebrations. Much of the food was symbolic, drawing them to worship the One who provided for all their needs.

And they used music. Music is woven all throughout the Bible. When the Israelites were finally and fully free of their slavery in

Egypt, Moses' sister Miriam sang, and other women danced with tambourines to praise God.[134] When the Israelites entered God's Promised Land, Jericho fell to the sound of horns.[135] Israel's first king, Saul, experienced the soothing effect of music, and there were musicians in the king's court.[136] King David was an expert songwriter,[137] and his skills as a musician are one of the first things we learn about him.[138] In the New Testament, music is mentioned far less, but it was still important. Jesus and the disciples sang a hymn; the apostle Paul and his fellow missionary Silas sang in jail.[139]

All creation reflects the God who made it. The Bible tells us that we are made in the image of God, and so our creativity, whatever that looks like, is us reflecting back who he is. This is worship.

Worship is the overflow of delight, of doing what we feel like we were made to do. Adam was made to worship; Eve was made to worship. The thumbnail moon in the velvet sky; the rising sun in the cotton-candy clouds; the hummingbird with his flurry of wings; the sunflower that turns her face to the sun; the elephant's trunk and the giraffe's eyelashes—these were made to worship as they do what they are made to do.

The secular becomes sacred when we act in a spirit of curiosity, care, creativity, and love. You were made for nothing less than a bright and colorful life made up of the wildest bouquet of these. Coming to the Bible with open hands helps us suddenly see all the ways our lives can live and breathe out God's heart into the world around us. The Bible isn't meant to be just something we read and then leave behind as we go about our days; it's our impetus to worship, helping us frame our days and everything we do. The Bible helps us see that from the very beginning, we were created to live our days in celebration and worship, to be mindful of God moving in our moments. These words help us orient our days to the grander Story.

Practice for Your Actual Life

What delights you? Take some time to consider it. Make a list.

Take a photo of something lovely. Write a poem that doesn't rhyme. Play a song on the piano or hum a tune in your car. Arrange flowers in a vase. Plant petunias in your flower bed. Sprinkle your creativity like confetti. You have been created by a Creator, and your creativity shows his spirit. This is worship.

Go for a walk. Feel your feet hit the sidewalk, feel your arms swing by your side. When you plant those petunias, feel the soil in your fingertips. Take a bite of a strawberry and notice the juice before you wipe it off your chin. Be still in the morning and hear the different voices of the songbirds, near and far, melodious and cawing. Make love to your spouse and delight in the good and lovely gift of intimacy explored in the right context. God gave you a body, mind, sense, and perception, and he created a million ways for you to use these things and enjoy them. This is worship.

Make eye contact with the people behind the counter at your favorite coffee shop. Learn their names and speak them. Have friends over for dinner. Enjoy their company. Leave your phone upstairs or in the car. Give the people you love your full attention, and listen like it matters. Be present. Be intentional.

Carry cash in your pocket so you can give it away. Partner with a trusted organization to sponsor a child or a school or a village. Use your resources—your time, skills, and money—to bring relief. Agree with God that human life and dignity are worth protecting, preserving, and prioritizing. This is worship.

Don't be distracted by your own makings so you miss out on the holy workmanship seated at your dinner table. Creation will never be more important than the Creator, and what God creates will always outdo what man has made. People matter more than product. Relationships matter more than sales goals. Prioritize connection over correction. Lead with love. This is worship.

At the end of the day, and—let's be real—sometimes right in the middle of it, rest. Take a nap. Take a break. Take a day. God gave you life and breath and work to do, but he did not create your work to be your undoing. Know when to stop. Set boundaries and margin. Be the master of your work—not the other way around. Rest. This is worship.

And while you are singing your songs, writing your memoirs, weeding your garden; while you are stirring your soup and tossing your salad and setting your table; while you are having sex or taking a nap—you are doing what you were made to do. And that is worship.

Take delight in the LORD, and he will give you your heart's desires.

PSALM 37:4, NLT

When you pray, dedicate your home, your yard, your bonus room and dishwasher and bicycle and garden to the King. As surely as you dedicate your heart to him, dedicate your front porch. Daily pledge every atom of every tool at your disposal to his good pleasure. It's all sacred anyway.

ANDREW PETERSON, *Adorning the Dark*

Together Work

That Time with the Loaves and the Fishes

COLLABORATION IS MY FAVORITE kind of work. I call it *Together Work*. Collaboration, partnering with someone who can bring their specific skills and gifts to the table, always makes me far more effective—in my writing, thinking, creating, parenting. In real terms, that "together work" happens in tangible ways: with my close friends as I verbally process the ideas I'm thinking about; with my husband as we talk through the needs, personalities, and learning styles of these boys we are raising into men; with my editor as she takes my mess and makes everything prettier. (Seriously. I do not want you to see what she has seen. She's a locked vault of my messy processes.)

Together Work always, always, always makes me better.

The Holy Spirit offers the most powerful kind of *Together Work*. If we have any hope of loving people who are hard to love; paying off debts that seem insurmountable; creating anything of value, including a book, a meal, a conversation, a person, then we need the Holy Spirit's partnership. I mean, we can do it ourselves, yes, usually. But partnering with the effectiveness of the Holy Spirit multiples *everything*. God can take what we do and do something with it that we could never imagine.

There are things we do every day that are *Together Work* with God. For me, writing is *Together Work*. The fact that I *want* to write is the work of God within me. When I physically sit down to write, this is *my work*. When something shows up on the page, this is *Together Work*. I mean, I don't know where the line is between his work and mine, but when someone reads what I have written and they are drawn to know God better, when they feel a pull to learn more about God and feel more able to live out the good and gracious things he has for them, then I know God and I have done *Together Work*. God can get his work done in me and through me because I was faithful to show up, sit still, listen, learn, write, teach. *Together Work*.

In this moment you are in right now, with this book in your hands, you are doing *Together Work*. Learning is *Together Work*. The fact that you *want* to read this book is God's doing. The fact that you *are* reading this book? That's your doing. Anything you learn from this book: you and God together. *Together Work*.

The reason we know the truth of *Together Work*, the reason we know it's possible and can be part of the fullness of our lives, is because of the Bible. I have fallen in love with the stories and examples of *Together Work* in the Bible. They start with small promptings, seemingly meaningless whispers, small nudges that might even be hard to pin down. But when people responded to God's prompting, he drew them into his larger story, even though they may have thought they were doing something simple, unrelated, impossible to be multiplied or magnified.

There's the famous story of when Jesus feeds five thousand people in an afternoon on a hillside.[140] Maybe it's because I am forever a hostess at heart, and wherever there is a party there is also food aplenty, or maybe it's just because I love when a story comes to life, especially when I can get into the minds of the characters. Either way, whether I'm thinking with my head, my heart, or my stomach, I dig this story of *Together Work*.

People followed Jesus everywhere he went. All the time, crowds of people trailed behind him, and I imagine they circled him on every side. Even when Jesus tried to get a little space to refuel, the people found him, surrounded him, and asked for more and more and more.

Straight from the top of this story, Jesus shows me that there comes a time when you've just got to step away. The people couldn't get enough of him and his firsthand miracles, and they followed him everywhere. He, the very one who could give them everything they wanted and needed, even he knew that he had to take care of himself. So he gathered the ones he trusted most, and he stepped away from the noise for a bit.

My introverted heart reads this and breathes a sigh of gratitude.

But then the crowds show up again, because *of course*. People from many towns ran ahead along the shore where he was traveling, always trying to anticipate his next move and be the first ones there. The writers tell us that the disciples came to Jesus and suggested he may want to send the people away to nearby farms and villages to get something to eat, and Jesus responded in classic fashion that makes me love him so much. I just have to wonder if there was a twinkle in his eye when he said, "You feed them."

"With what?" they protested, pointing out that catering for this many would require months of wages.

In one of the retellings, Jesus asks Philip, "Where can we buy bread to feed all these people?" It's one of the earliest story problems. Jesus knows the answer, and he already has a plan. He gives Philip the chance to be the hero with the right answer, but Philip kind of misses the whole question. Jesus asks where they can buy bread, but Philip jumps straight to how much it would cost to feed this whole party crew.

Jesus asks them, "How much bread do you have?"

They came back and reported, "There's a young boy here with five barley loaves and two fish. But what good is that with this huge crowd?"

A fair question, gentlemen; a fair question, indeed. The text states that there were five thousand men present, and that doesn't count the women and children. (In Jewish culture of the day, men and women usually ate separately, and the children ate with the women.) So, the total number of hungry people may have actually been ten to fifteen thousand.[141] Five loaves and two fish? Hardly enough.

The writers tell us, "Then Jesus took the loaves, gave thanks to God, and distributed them to the people. Afterward he did the same with the fish. And they all ate as much as they wanted."

Jesus multiplied five loaves and two fish to feed more than five thousand people. What they originally gave him seemed insufficient, which is basically how I feel every time I give something to God. I'm always like, "Well, I don't know what this is yet or how you can possibly do something with my feeble attempts here, but you can have it." The crazy thing? In his hands, what we give him is always enough. We feel that our contribution is inadequately meager, but he can use it. In ways we cannot imagine, he multiplies exponentially.

But even with that long list of things I'm learning, we haven't yet talked about my favorite part, my favorite character, because she's actually not even listed in the story.

Somewhere behind the story of when Jesus fed five thousand, there's a mom who packed a simple lunch for her son. And that, that right there, is my favorite part. The *Together Work*.

Somewhere in the hidden history of Bible times, a mom packed a simple lunch for her son before he left home that morning. She was taking care of her boy, and she couldn't know that Jesus would turn that silent work of her hands, the supplies from her kitchen, and her faithful love for her son, into one of his greatest miracles. Don't miss it, moms and dads, especially you who are tired and unnoticed. You just never know what he's up to with the little somethings you have to give, the lunches you pack on the early mornings when you think nobody is even awake enough to notice.

○────○

The Bible is filled with stories like this one, of people who did the right thing because it was the next thing, of people who partnered with God in what he was doing because they gave him the work of their hands.

Consider Mary, the sister of Lazarus and Martha, who poured her expensive perfume over Jesus' feet while he was eating in Simon's home.[142] The disciples were indignant, saying what a waste it was, how the perfume could have been sold at a high price, the money given to the poor. Jesus has many answers for them—not the least of which are "stop criticizing her." But then he makes this puzzling statement: "She has poured this perfume on me to prepare my body for burial."[143]

That statement had to raise some eyebrows. The guys at that dinner party didn't know that Jesus would be arrested, put on trial, and killed within one week. Most beautiful of all, Mary didn't know that either. She poured her expensive perfume on the Messiah who was alive, unaware that her perfume was a foreshadowing act of all that was to come. She simply followed the prompting in her spirit, went to the dinner, and poured out her perfume because that was how her heart longed to worship: by giving all she had with heartfelt love. *Together Work.*

In the early Old Testament, there is an obscure character, hardly mentioned at all. His name is Bezalel. He shows up amid chapters and books filled with so many careful instructions on the making of all the tangible things for God's interactions with his people: the Tabernacle, the Ark of the Covenant, and the Holy Place. Suddenly, God brought forth Bezalel, whom he had specifically chosen. Moses said, "The LORD has filled Bezalel with the Spirit of God, giving him great wisdom, ability, and expertise in all kinds of crafts."[144]

What kinds of crafts? Well, for one, Bezalel made the special curtain that hung in the Tabernacle, this intricately woven cloth of blue, purple, and scarlet threads. And it's important to note here that this was no small curtain. The instructions read, "Make the Tabernacle from ten curtains of finely woven linen. . . . These ten curtains must all be exactly the same size—42 feet long and 6 feet wide. Join five of these curtains together to make one long curtain, then join the other five into a second long curtain. . . . Then make fifty gold clasps and fasten the long curtains together with the clasps. In this way, the Tabernacle will be made of one continuous piece."[145]

The curtain divided the two sacred rooms, the Holy Place and the Most Holy Place, and this curtain symbolized how the people were separated from God because of their sin.

When we look ahead to the story of the night that Jesus hung from the cross, in the very moment that he died, "the curtain in the sanctuary of the Temple was torn in two, from top to bottom."[146] No man could have reached the top of that heavy curtain and done such vandalism as to rip it in two; not a person on earth was strong enough to do that. That's why God tells us that it was torn from the top. He tore it—because everything humanity knew about meeting God had just changed.

I had once thought the curtain was torn in grief, agony, and sadness, but now I see: The curtain was torn to show that there was no longer a separation between God and his people. The blood of Jesus had torn the veil—the curtain Bezalel had made!

This reality is so profound to me. I promise you, it keeps me awake at night. Why? Because we artists can get a little too precious with our work. We can get so caught up in what we're making, so possessive of it, so careful that only people who appreciate it are the ones who get to see it, read it, watch it, enjoy it. We're needy like that.

If Bezalel had been too precious with his curtain, too sacred with his own work, too careful or too possessive of it, he couldn't have been in the *Together Work* of redemption. God knew Bezalel would have the wisdom to see that his art could be a sacrifice. It became something that the people of God could forever look to, the barrier that came down, torn apart from the top. And it's the same for us: Whatever we offer to God with open hands can be poured out, used up, and even damaged—because we don't know what God will ultimately do with our *Together Work*.

o———o

Seeking to fall in love with the Bible in our actual lives is *Together Work*. Our work looks like this: It is the tangible work of our hands and our time. It is in the choices to obey, to do the right thing, to love the person in front of us. Our work happens when we show up to read the Bible, to meditate on what we're learning, to memorize words and sew them into our memory. It is in our actions of studying, journaling, and reading. It is in the discipline of prayer, of repentance. It's in the open dialogue of creativity, conversation, and small acts of courage. It's in allowing ourselves rest so we're not too tired to work at all.

God's work often looks like this: It's the hidden work that we cannot see. It's invisible, silent, and subtle. It happens behind the scenes and beneath the soil. It's the gift of healing and forgiveness, of answered prayers and restored relationships. It is in the renewal of rest, when we can't explain why we feel better—we just do. His work is in the wisdom of the moment, when he shows up to give us strength, favor, effectiveness, and the influence that only he can reach.

When we show up to do our work, we make space for God to do his.

When we make ourselves available, he makes himself accessible. *Together Work.*

Practice for Your Actual Life

In the Old Testament, David triumphed over Goliath with a sling and a stone, but he didn't start out killing giants. David said, "Don't worry about this Philistine. I'll go fight him! I have been taking care of my father's sheep and goats, . . . rescu[ing] [them] from . . . lions and bears. The LORD who rescued me from the claws of the lion and the bear will rescue me from this Philistine!"[147] He was faithful to what was in front of him, he kept doing the next thing, and God used what he offered to defeat an army.

Or how about Mary, who was young, poor, and female, all the qualities that deemed her worthless in the culture of her time. And yet God chose her for the most important role in the history of humanity. Sometimes we can forget that a young, unmarried girl who became pregnant risked absolute disaster in that day. If her father rejected her, she could be forced into begging or prostitution to earn a living for herself and her child; unless the father of the child agreed to marry her, she would probably remain unmarried for life. And Mary, with her story about becoming pregnant by the Holy Spirit, risked being considered crazy on top of it all. Still, when the angel Gabriel appeared to tell her she would carry this child, she said, "May everything you have said about me come true."[148] She didn't yet know the tremendous opportunity in front of her, nor the unimaginable pain. We can imagine her peers would ridicule her, and we know that her son would be rejected and murdered—but also, she would be praised for every generation to come, and her submission to the journey would bring about the salvation of the world. She couldn't have known all of this when she said yes. She only knew that God was asking her to serve him, and she obeyed. In her words to Gabriel, I hear her saying, "Let's do this."

The Bible helps us see how these stories aren't extraordinary people doing extraordinary things, but rather people just like us working together with an extraordinary God. The Holy Spirit offers us the same opportunities today—beginning with helping us "want to." When you're reluctant, or afraid, or intimidated, he can put a desire to *want to* within you. If you don't have the "want to," ask God for it. *God, I want to want to.*

Ask for that blessing, that he will give you the gift of *Together Work* in your conversations, your marriage, your parenting, your teaching, your writing, your spending, your giving, your love. Everything is more when God is your collaborative partner.

Make me faithful to my craft . . .
Let me be diligent to the discipline and
the labor required, but let me never
forget that all such measured faithfulness
yields only a polished stone, meaningless
until it is stirred from within by your breath,
until it is set by you in a crown of your own crafting.

DOUGLAS MCKELVEY, *Every Moment Holy*

CHAPTER 13

Quicksand

When You Know Just What to Say

I REALLY THOUGHT quicksand would be a much bigger obstacle in life. There was so much talk about quicksand in my childhood— it was forever showing up in storybooks and movies—so I guess I always thought it would be a sizable danger in adulthood. But I have yet to encounter quicksand.

Same is true for catching on fire. So much discussion and practice of stop, drop, and roll. I thought people catching flame would be far more prevalent.

Also, drugs on the playground. I was definitely prepared to "just say no," but I haven't encountered that warned-of endless parade of people lurking in dark alleys and candy stores, trying to make me consume drugs and cigarettes.

I had a significant fear of moving out West, because I thought they still solved issues with duels. Thankfully I wasn't born two hundred years ago, in a little tiny ghost town with dusty streets, because I didn't know how I'd ever survive all the pistols waving around.

The thing is, "telling someone about Jesus" fell into this same category of misplaced expectations. You guys, I was trained—hard core. There is a color pattern seared into my brain: black, red, blue, white, green, gold, each color with meaning and a line in the script on the path of the Romans Road to "lead a person to the Lord." The beaded bracelet, the Wordless Book, and even a random memory of an odd clown made of yarn, just in case I wanted to use his arms and legs as prompts for conversation.

(These may be the roots of why I feel uncomfortable with simplified formulas, overused clichés, easy answers, and awkward conversations. I did not want to approach anyone with my colorful bracelet, my construction paper booklet, or—dear heavens—a loopy, yarn clown and tell them how to live their life and plan their afterlife.)

I was trained for these discussions, but nobody ever asked me these questions in my actual life. Nobody wanted to talk about these things. These strategies fell into the same category as quicksand, catching on fire, and ghost-town pistols. I felt ready to give an answer, but nobody was asking.

So imagine my surprise when one of my dearest friends pulled up a chair at a wedding reception and said, "Tricia, I want to talk about your new book. I have so many questions about the Bible."

Why did my stomach drop? Why do I find that question so intimidating?

First of all, I didn't really know how to talk about this book yet. Aside from saying, "I'm writing a book about loving the Bible in your actual life," I didn't know how to talk about *this book* without sounding like a weirdo-Christian selling salvation door to door, persisting even if the sign on the door says No Solicitors.

I am not a salesman. Seriously, if you don't want it, I won't push it. I'm just not made that way. Which makes me a not-so-great bookseller, and an even-less-great evangelist. I can't convince anyone to buy my books, and I can't convince anyone that God is real. You have to taste and see for yourself.

But there I sat, with just a few minutes to say so many things to the dearest friend of my soul: (*a*) about my new book, (*b*) which is about falling in love with the Bible, (*c*) while I suspect this isn't a book she will want to read. She and I are cut from the same cloth, but we have never practiced the same faith. We have quietly respected each other's separate lanes on the shared highway of life.

And then she said, "My daughter goes to a Christian school now, so the Bible is part of our evening homework. I have never read this stuff before, and I have so many questions. Basically, can you tell me this: Why did Jesus die on the cross? I mean, I get that he did, but why?"

(*Dear God, she's going straight for the jugular.*) I looked casual, but I was praying like crazy. (*God, I'm going to need you to answer for me. In me. Through me. This is your territory. If you've ever given me words, I need them now. Amen and amen.*)

Here was a real, live person wanting to talk about the greatest foundation of my faith—*she* asked *me*. And she was not just any random person on the sidewalk of life but a real person who really matters to me. She wanted to know why Jesus died on the cross and why it should matter to her.

I said, "Well, back then, there were hundreds of rules to follow, every minute of every day. Each rule was supposed to keep people close to God, and anytime someone broke a rule, the only way to get back on track with God was to kill an animal. There was this crazy-complicated system of animal blood in exchange for forgiveness. Forgiveness required blood to be poured out. So they had to keep track of all the things they had done wrong, all the sins they had committed, and they needed to report that list to the priest. He would tell them how many animals they needed to sacrifice to get right with God, in order to get a clean slate."

"That's a lot of animals," she said.

"And a lot of blood. It was an exhausting way to live, forever keeping rules, keeping score, keeping track. But then God offered a new plan, and instead of killing all the animals and pouring out their blood, he offered the blood of his own son, Jesus."

She nodded like this made sense, so I forged ahead.

"Jesus said, 'I'm going to do this one time, as a blood sacrifice for everything you have ever done and anything you will ever do. My blood will be enough, from this day forward.' All of that rule keeping? It's finished. All of the animal killing? It's finished. And if you choose to believe that his blood is enough to get you right with God, then you can live with me forever."

My friend looked at me for a moment, completely still. Then she said, "Why didn't anyone ever tell me this?"

(*Actually,* I thought, *that was easier to say than I ever imagined it would be.*)

"So that's why he died? That's how it works?"

"That's how it works. And that's eternal life. If you choose to believe you can't get to heaven on your own, and if you believe that the blood of Jesus is the way, then he offers you eternal life. And believing is enough. And I have to tell you, when you put your faith there, there is nothing left to be afraid of. Including death. It has no hold on you."

She said, "What about my husband? He has so many questions. I don't know if he will buy into this."

"Honestly," I said, "I get that. Salvation by faith in Christ sounds too easy. It feels like we should have to do something to save ourselves, right? People like to make religion much harder than it is, a path of beating ourselves up and earning our way. Anything else feels too easy, but Jesus made it clear—it's the only way. That decision for your husband, well, it's up to him and God. Faith means we get to make our own decision, and we can't make it for anyone else."

I told her that I think often about a thief who was crucified next to Jesus, who spoke to him in the final moments of that last hour of his life. We don't know very much about his story. What we do know is this: In that very last moment, as he himself was dying, that man put his faith in Jesus, and then Jesus said, "You will be with me."[149] I told my friend that I've thought often about the thief's family, how they may have not come, or may have been too ashamed to stand close enough to hear that last-minute conversation. Perhaps his family thought that he died as a thief unforgiven, a guy who had done his own thing for all his days and now finished his life without any faith. And perhaps they did have faith themselves, and they didn't know until they got to heaven and looked around—that there he was, waiting for them.

That's convicting to me. How many people have I made that assumption about? Believing that they died without knowing Jesus? I don't know what conversation they are having with the Holy Spirit. I don't know what is happening between them and God, because it's not actually my business. It's between them and God.

My friend could also make this decision on her own, and she could change the course of her life—and beyond.

I wanted to be careful as I talked about the word *faith*. Faith isn't something we have to accomplish to earn a ticket to heaven. If that were the case, then faith would be just one more thing we have to do, back to that list of rules to follow. Human actions can never save us—not even our own efforts to believe with all our might.

Faith is a gift God gives us because he is saving us. In this grandest mercy that blows my mind, he gives us faith.

If you're new to the Bible, new to these questions about God— do you feel a tug in your heart to ask more questions, to learn more? It's the whisper of the Holy Spirit giving you a gift of belief. He's inviting you into a relationship, one where you are endlessly loved and become like him. Through the faith he gives us, he bridges the gap between a sinful people and a sinless God, and he carries us from death into life.

Your part is simply to open your hands. Let him plant the seed of faith within your heart.

The conversation with my dear girl unfolded in a moment in our actual lives. For just a few fleeting moments, I told her the core of everything I believe, the scarlet thread that weaves the Bible together, from the front to the back, from creation to eternity. It was a holy moment on sacred ground, just before we got pulled onto the dance floor for a rousing rendition of "Paradise by the Dashboard Light."

When we read the Bible, when we discover who Jesus really is in the pages, we can find the real answer about life and faith—and, ready to give a real answer when we're asked. Not a memorized line, not a script to follow, not contrived words that feel stiff and impersonal. But a truth that has sunk into our bones. The Bible is for each one of us, and when we know that, we can share that truth with somebody else.

○——————○

Have you ever gotten one of those creditor's checks in the mail, the kind that's ostensibly made out for tens of thousands of dollars? I have. And it looks so good at first. Addressed to me, made out to me, all for *me*. A glance at a check like that makes the mind spin and the heart stir. All I have to do is sign it, and everyone's Christmases and college educations will be paid for? *Quick*, I think. *Somebody hand me a pen.*

But then I realize that "they" didn't sign it. They, the anonymous philanthropists and creditors who promised me all the money, are waiting for me to sign the check. They're waiting for me to make a promise to myself, to sign on the line and become indebted to them. I could have all the money, but I'm only borrowing it. I have to pay it all back—or I become their slave.

Instead of signing the check, I exhale in resignation and indignation. That kind of money wouldn't be mine, not on these terms, not on this day. I write in bold letters across the front: VOID.

Because when someone writes a check that cannot be used, you must write the word VOID across the face of the check to make sure nobody tries to spend what isn't really in the account. No matter the amount written in the box and on the line, that check is now worth nothing. It's like millions of Monopoly dollars. It comes up empty. Returned void.

The Bible says that the Word of God *does not return void*. And I had never really understood that term before, *return void*. I mean, I understand what both words mean, separately, but together it sounds like some kind of King James language that nobody uses anymore.

But as I stared at one of those checks, suddenly that phrase, those words, *return void*—it all made sense to me.

When the Bible says those words, I can have confidence that it's not a scam. It's not a trick. And it will never come up empty. Because, you see, when I study Scripture, I am making an investment. I store it in my heart and my mind. Scripture is full of deeper truths that influence me exactly where I am, shining a light into my anxiety, my hurt, my fear, my relationships, and my choices. Even if I read something that seems to not apply to me, something that makes little sense to me, something that raises more questions than answers—it is not empty. It fits under the category of "maybe not today," not under the blanket of "this doesn't apply at all." The words are not meaningless. They will return to me in a moment when I need them. The words will show up in my mind when I need comfort or clarity. The principles become a building block for something I will learn later, something I couldn't have understood if I hadn't learned this first. The Word of God does not return void. There is something in it, the seed of something I can take to the bank, so to speak.

God will use his words in your life however he chooses, and it's exciting to get to watch for the ways he'll meet you there. His words matter. They have deep meaning. They do not return void.

As I sat down to write this book about falling in love with the Bible, I felt daunted. I started spilling with notes and ideas, revelations and discoveries, stories and ideas. But instead of feeling joy and anticipation, I felt anxiety. God's words are so vast and deep and full, so much bigger than anything I could possibly hold or put on a page—and so, holding my thoughts has felt like wrestling with a giant bouquet of helium balloons in a windstorm.

But God's words are—this Word is—not mine to control or wrestle. All I've been asked to do is offer what I have, a few of the ways God has met me in the pages of the Bible, and where he might just want to meet you as well. Falling in love with the Bible isn't a straight line, a checklist, a clearly charted path. So in these pages, I hope I can give you just a glimpse, a taste of how God's words aren't just for a church service or to be left on a shelf—they are living and breathing in our actual lives.

Here's what I want you to know, beloved and anonymous friend of mine: Spending time in the Word of God is never, ever wasted. It's a blank check that keeps multiplying, with zeroes and commas, and it's signed. God has signed it. He always delivers on his promises. And because of that, his book has something in it for you and for me, no matter what we're facing that day or what friendship might be falling apart or what fear might be eating away at us. He will meet us in the pages, even if we don't recognize him at the time.

I can't make any promises that aren't mine. But the beauty of it is this: The words aren't mine. The promises aren't mine. They're his.

He invites us to come to him, and he calls us to abide in him. That means get close and stay closer still. He promises that time with him, time spent looking for him and finding him, will never be a waste. Let's hold on to this promise with both hands: Spending time with God is never, ever wasted. God said it, and I'm banking on it.

○———○

I realize it's still possible that you may be reading this and wondering if God's words are really, truly *for you*. It's possible that you are self-selecting yourself right out of this promise, for any number of reasons.

"I'm not from a religious family."

"I don't even own a Bible."

"I'm not in the in-crowd."

"I didn't even grow up in the church."

Listen, I get it. We have all seen how Christianity can feel like a club you have to join, and if you don't know the passwords and you can't speak the language, then you're forever on the outside. The list of people who have felt this way is endless, and even the most devout Christians can trace their lineage back to a time when they were on the outside looking in.

I am compelled by—what is the word I want? Touched. Captivated. Drawn to. I am (all of these words)—the passage where Solomon prayed for the foreigners who will hear of the love of God, even though they were not in the "in-crowd" of Israelites, the original chairmen of the club.

Solomon prayed, "They will come from distant lands when they hear of your great name and your strong hand and your powerful arm." He asks God to hear their prayer and grant what they ask, and "in this way, all the people of the earth will come to know you and fear you, just as your own people Israel do."[150]

The foreigners. That's me. My family. My community. And it may very well be you too. We are not from the line of Jacob. We are not chosen people by lineage or heredity or genetics. In every sense that Solomon had in mind, we are outsiders who have heard of God's great name, his powerful arm, his strong hand. Solomon prayed for me and you that day, asking God to hear from heaven.

May we never forget that there was a time when we were on the outside, looking in. And the pages of the Bible are sprinkled with people who changed lanes because they wanted what God offers, and to be honest, some of them slipped in under the wire. We see throughout the Bible that people regardless of background had the opportunity to join the story. So even if you, reader, feel like you're not from the right background or you've done things that mean you can't be included—you can be.

When Moses was leading the Israelites out of Egypt, after the plagues of frogs and locusts and rivers of blood and the deaths of firstborn sons, Pharaoh finally pointed his finger to the boundary line and said, "Get *out!*" And the people left so fast that they didn't have time for their bread to rise. Tucked into that part of the story is this: "That night the people of Israel left Rameses and started for Succoth. There were about 600,000 men, plus all the women and children. *A rabble of non-Israelites went with them, along with great flocks and herds of livestock.*"[151]

(My own emphasis added, because I love italics and because this deserves to be pointed out.)

A rabble is a mob. Can't you just picture it? A "mob" of people—all of whom seemed to be uninvited, excluded, unchosen, and left out—decided they wanted in on this. They slipped in with the crowd, to be among those who escaped Egypt just in time. I imagine them saying, "I want to go where they are going. I want what they have. I want to follow their God. Take me with you! I am out of here! I'm following that guy and his God."

And they followed Moses right out of Egypt, from the scene of the plagues, straight into the dry land of the Red Sea. They didn't start out on his team, but these people wanted to follow this God who was clearly in charge. I love to imagine them tagging along with God's people, feeling like they had escaped under the wire.

And if all of this still feels like it still can't be about you or for you, then let me give you this:

Jesus said, "I was found by people who were not looking for me. I showed myself to those who were not asking for me."[152]

And also this: "Those who were not my people, I will now call my people. And I will love those whom I did not love before. . . . at the place where they were told, 'you are not my people,' there they will be called 'children of the living God.'"[153]

(That's you.)

Practice for Your Actual Life

Sometimes people whose stories are told in the Bible followed God with bold, loud decisions. Like Saul in the New Testament, the most unlikely to ever change his mind and follow Christ. He hated people who followed Jesus and was literally killing the early believers—until he encountered Jesus Christ personally. He acknowledged Jesus as Lord, confessed his own sin, surrendered his life to Christ, and resolved to follow him in everything he did. He immediately went to the synagogue to tell the Jews about Jesus Christ.[154] He wasted no time, and he was loud about it.

Or let's look at the woman at the well. She was a Samaritan, so she was a member of a shunned mixed race; it seems she was known for what might have been a promiscuous lifestyle, with a series of many men in her life; and she was drawing water at the well in the middle of the day, all to avoid talking to people who knew her reputation. And along comes Jesus, inviting her out of the lifestyle she's in and into relationship with him. What does she do? The woman leaves her water jar beside the well and runs back to the village, telling everyone to come and see him.[155] Come meet this man who is a Rule Changer. She was loud about it.

But other people were quiet in their decision. Nicodemus was afraid anyone would see him having a conversation with Jesus, but Nicodemus had some real questions. He wanted to learn, so he made an appointment with Jesus undercover, in the dark of night. We know very little about this man, such was his quiet decision, but we know that he left that evening's encounter changed. He made a bold move, risking everything, but keeping it all to himself—between him and Jesus.[156]

Joseph of Arimathea, another Jewish religious leader, was a secret disciple of Jesus, because he was afraid of his judge-y Pharisee friends. When Jesus had died and hung lifeless on the cross, Joseph asked permission to take down Jesus' body. When Pilate gave permission, Joseph came and took the body away, and—get *this*—it says, "with him came Nicodemus, the man who had come to Jesus at night."[157] Together they followed the Jewish burial custom, wrapping Jesus' body with spice in long sheets of linen cloth. Joseph donated the tomb where Jesus was buried,[158] and he kept his faithfulness a secret from his friends.

Not everybody was loud about their relationship with Jesus. You don't have to be, either. You don't have to tell everybody. You don't have to find a church to attend this Sunday so you can march down the aisle and "declare your decision." You don't have to update your Facebook profile to state your religious views. You can be quiet and personal. You can tell everyone, or you can tell nobody. You are allowed to tell only Jesus.

You don't have to follow Jesus loudly, just faithfully. Be ready for the moments he brings to you, the conversations he invites you to, and the people he gives you to love.

Our God specializes in finding and changing people who believe themselves to be out of reach. Choose quietly, or choose out loud.

But please: Choose this day.

All human beings have some knowledge of God available to them. At some level, they have an indelible sense that they need something or someone who is on a higher plane and infinitely greater than they are. Prayer is seeking to respond and connect to that being and reality . . . All prayer is responding to God. In all cases God is the initiator—"hearing" always precedes asking. God comes to us first or we would never reach out to him.

TIMOTHY KELLER, *Prayer*

Epilogue

AN INSTRUCTOR ONCE TOLD ME about this master teacher who invited her students into her home each week. She would open this giant book, and every week she and her students would dive into a passage, pore over the commentaries, and interact, wrestle, and debate with what they were learning and how it inspired them. This sounds like my kind of event, and I drooled over the very idea.

Late one night, three of the students were walking home together, and one of the students said to the other two, "I feel like I owe you two an apology. Clearly I spoke with the teacher all evening, and neither of you got a word in. That was very selfish of me, and I am so sorry."

The second student said, "Are you kidding me? What are you talking about? Obviously, I am the one who monopolized the conversation. I'm the one who had the full attention of the teacher, and I am the one who should apologize."

And the third student said, "Wait. I feel like I'm the one who should say I'm sorry. I took all of her time and attention tonight."

And then the three fell silent in this shared moment together, as they realized what had happened: They each received what they needed, the wisdom they had asked for, the connection they longed for.

And so it is, when we open the pages of the Bible and spend time with the divine spirit who meets us in the pages. Each one of us can read this living Word and feel as though the Spirit is speaking directly to us, just to us, only to us.

I am a notetaker, and I process my thoughts through my pen on the page. So when I'm learning, I want to write it down. It's maybe a little obsessive on my part, like sometimes I can feel like I haven't really learned something unless I have written it down.

I once sat in a writing class, and as the professor was teaching, I learned the way I learn: I was furiously taking notes. Downright scribbling.

She walked past me, put her hand on my arm, and said, "Tricia, when you walk in the mist, you will get wet."

I nodded knowingly, but inside my head, I was like, *Mmmm, okay, Yoda. I don't really know what that means, but I'll write it down.*

She interrupted my note-taking with her hand on my arm again, and she said, "You're trying to catch it all, like rain in a bucket. But learning doesn't work that way. It's like a mist that settles on your clothes. You can't catch all the ideas, but if you stay with it, they become part of you. If you walk in the mist, you'll discover you have gotten wet."

I still wrote it down. Because I'm a freethinking rebel with a pen in her hand.

But she did have a strong point, and obviously it stayed with me.

When I'm studying the Bible, I can feel compelled to chase after it, to read all the commentaries, to take all the classes, to catch all the drops of rain in my bucket. It's a noble cause and a worthy goal, and people indeed spend their lives on this very pursuit. But also, there is much to be said about the beauty of how the disciples learned: They walked with Jesus, talked with him, and listened. He became part of them; his spirit saturated theirs.

As we wrap up these pages together, please know: This book is in no way intended to be a substitute for the real thing. It's merely a companion for you, stories and insights about how God has met me over and over as I've read, studied, learned, memorized, and meditated on his words. Consider this to be simply one of the lights on the floor aisle of the movie theater or the airplane, a lamp strategically placed to point you to the greater path to safety.

I have not loved the Bible all my life, but I have always respected everything about it. My devotion was born of a ten-year journey of knowing that I needed both incredible wisdom and miraculous help to get through the challenges coming my way at high speeds, intense velocity, and unstoppable momentum. And along the way of walking in a foggy mist, I have gotten wet.

May it be so for you, my friend. May your appetite ever increase for more of the real thing, to know this Jesus who became human and moved into the neighborhood, who invites us to know him, to do life with him, to become as he is in our actual lives.

This book is for you.

Pay close attention to what you hear. The closer you listen, the more understanding you will be given—and you will receive even more. To those who listen to my teaching, more understanding will be given.
MARK 4:24-25, NLT

Fifteen Things to Know as You Navigate the Bible

1. Make it yours. Write all over it, if that's your style. (It's definitely my style.) An unopened Bible doesn't help anyone at all, and as we've well established: This Book Is for You. So grab your pens and make it yours.

2. Never let yourself feel embarrassed to open to the table of contents. While it may seem like the people around you know right where to turn, I can promise you there are other people who are quietly trying to figure out the Old Testament from the New, the left from the right, the Gospels from the letters. Do yourself a favor and make the table of contents your friend. We don't expect ourselves or anyone else to be able to navigate other giant anthologies without a table of contents, and that's because page numbers never hurt anybody.

3. The Bible has two parts: the Old Testament and the New Testament. You could remember these as the Old Promises and the New Promises.

4. The Old Testament is the first part of the Bible, and it tells the story of God's original promise to his people. It has a deep history of the nation of Israel, and the teachings of

prophets who proclaimed the consequences of not living by the truths and expectations of God. There were many rules and expectations, and they were very laborious to maintain.

5. The New Testament is the second part of the Bible, and it explains how everything changed after Jesus was born into the world. Jesus replaced the hundreds of rules with one big one: Love God and love people. Anyone who believes that Jesus is the Son of God, that his blood is enough to cover our many sins, can have a relationship with him.

6. The Bible is organized with this formula: *Book Chapter: Verse*. If you want to look up Genesis 1:1, you'll open to the book of Genesis, turn to the first chapter, and point to the first verse. If you want to look up John 3:16, you'll open to the book of John, turn to the third chapter, and find the sixteenth verse. Chapters are usually arranged with numbers in a larger font, while verses are usually numbered with small font within the text.

7. The Bible consists of sixty-six books and letters, and they each have a name and a purpose. They are not placed in the order in which they were written—unless you purchase a chronological Bible, which I have come to deeply enjoy. Sometimes it's really nice to read a story from beginning to end, and that perspective can give us new eyes to understand the story.

8. In the back of your Bible, you'll likely find a concordance, or an index, which will help you find a few verses that contain a specific word or theme in the Bible. Thanks to the conveniences of the internet, we can also do a quick search to find subjects and verses that refer to a topic or person of the Bible.

9. There are many translations written of the entire Bible, using older language or more modern phrases and word choices. There is no single "best" translation, so you have the freedom to choose one that feels comfortable to you. (However, steer away from niche Bibles with Disney characters on the cover, or with titles that include special audiences like "cat lovers" or "soccer players" and what have you. I have nothing against cat lovers or soccer players, but the Word of God is specifically for *everyone*. If the book cover narrows the audience, it may not be a reliable version.)

10. Before you study your Bible, begin by praying. Ask God to open your eyes, to give you spiritual understanding, and to teach you what he wants you to know. He wants us to know him.

11. Choose one book to study. If you're beginning for the first time, start with the book of John or the book of James. Over the course of several days, read through the entire book, and let yourself do this more than once. As you read, themes and ideas will jump out at you each time. Timothy Keller describes meditation as "thinking in the presence of God."[159] Meditate on what you read by writing it down. This allows an opportunity for God's Word to speak to you personally.

12. Slow down and focus verse by verse, breaking down the text word by word. If you like, use dictionaries, commentaries, and study Bibles to aid in your understanding (but don't let other sources become a substitute for the real thing in your life). God's Word is alive, so you can study the same passage several times and continue to discover something new in each layer.

13. Read at your own pace. Once you've finished one book of the Bible, choose another. Spend as much time as you like digging into the longer books of the Bible. Don't rush yourself to read with someone else's timing. This Book is for you, and the time you spend in these pages are for you and God. Show up, and take your time.

14. Don't just study God's Word for the sake of reading it. Put it into practice in your life. When God speaks to you personally through the application principles you find on the page, look for ways to put these words to action in your life. Don't just read it: Do it.

15. Keep after it. There is no limit to the understanding, growth, and learning that can come from your time spent in the pages of God's words.

Acknowledgments

Emily Nagoski and Amelia Nagoski wrote that "there is a distinct downside to effort that is too effortless: When a task feels easy, we feel more confident about our ability to perform that task even though we are actually *more likely to fail*."[160] In fact, beginners who are *thoroughly incompetent* rate themselves as *very confident* in their ability to do a thing they've just learned to do, while experts know how difficult their work is, so they tend to rate their abilities as moderate. Essentially, the greater the task, the deeper you dive, and the harder it feels, the more acquainted you become with how much you don't know.

I have learned that this dichotomy is especially healthy if you're writing a book about the Bible. Don't get overly confident in writing about a topic to which theologians and scholars and academicians devote their entire lifetime studies, in its countless, endless, organic intricacies. I'm not saying don't do it; I'm saying don't imagine it will be easy or that you will in any way feel like an expert.

This has been the most challenging book I have ever written. The deeper I explored writing a book about the Bible, the more I learned about how little I know. The more I study, the more I realize I am only getting started. I don't know all there is to know about the Bible—I only know how to love it. And even that felt stretched to a near breaking point during a few miles along the way.

There even came a time—very late in the game—when my manuscript became irrevocably lost in what can only be explained as a divine intervention. When all the Microsoft experts and Genius Bar associates cannot explain what happened, one must consider a supernatural authority may have intercepted a project that *should not* go into the world. I let myself throw a fit, and then I got back to work. God's "no" is as important as his "yes," and I wanted nothing to do with a book he didn't want written. So I began anew. I think I wrote the length of this book three times in order to create what you hold in your hands.

That kind of writing and rewriting has caused me to question my direction to profound degrees. My writing studio is decoupaged with Post-it notes of people whose names belong on billboards across the land.

I thank Greg Johnson, my literary agent and friend, the first one who said, "I think you should write a book about falling in love with the Bible. That's what the world really needs, and you're the writer to do it." Greg, you are forever my champion, stretching me to do the next big thing.

I thank Lynne Rumsey, the math genius in my life, who turned even the absurdity of my legalism into an algebraic equation to show how impossible it is to craft a life deserving of God's faithfulness and favor. You are the most generous person I know, an incarnate algorithm of friendship, grace, and loyalty.

I thank my mom and dad, who have gently let the tables turn. After decades of teaching me to love learning, now they sit together and read my words aloud, letting me teach them what I have learned to love.

I thank Caitlyn Carlson, for making a castle out of my pile

of wet sand. I thank Elizabeth Schroll, for combing through my words to brush out all the tangles. Thank you both for holding my hand through the labor of this birth.

I thank my husband Peter, who keeps me fueled with forehead kisses, cups of coffee, and endless dialogues about the ideas, stories, metaphors, and theologies I'm thinking through. Peter suggested just last week, "Since you're almost finished with this one, may I suggest a narrower topic for the next book? I propose a book titled *How to Make Popsicles.*"

I thank you, the readers, who gather my words in your basket and then sprinkle them along your path for others to find as well. Thank you for joining me on the page, for letting me learn out loud, and for permitting me to make up new words when all the others just won't do. Writers need readers; God gave me you.

We have talked about the Bible, how *This Book Is for You.*

And now, it's important that I tell you, this small creation is too.

Notes

EPIGRAPH

1. Andy Stanley first taught me the wisdom of these words, and I have prayed them over my sons each night, since before they could understand them. For more on his words on wisdom, read *The Best Question Ever: A Revolutionary Approach to Decision Making* (Sisters, OR: Multnomah Books, 2004).

INTRODUCTION

2. To quote John Lewis. "Never, ever be afraid to make some noise and get in good trouble, necessary trouble" (tweet from June 2018).
3. Acts 17:27.
4. Lin-Manuel Miranda, "The Room Where It Happens," *Hamilton* © 2015 Atlantic Records.
5. Martha Beck, *Leaving the Saints: How I Lost the Mormons and Found My Faith* (New York: Three Rivers Press, 2005), dedication.

CHAPTER 1: LET'S START AT THE VERY BEGINNING

6. Acts 17:28.
7. Psalm 90:4.
8. "Who Wrote the Book of Genesis?" *ZA Blog*, August 31, 2018, https://zondervanacademic.com/blog/who-wrote-genesis.
9. Ark Encounter, "Was Noah's Ark Found on Mount Ararat?" accessed January 22, 2021, https://arkencounter.com/noahs-ark/found/.
10. Got Questions, "Is the Book of Job a True Story or a Parable/Allegory?" accessed January 22, 2021, gotquestions.org/Job-true-story.html.
11. John D. Morris, "Did Jonah Really Get Swallowed by a Whale?" Institute for Creation Research, December 1, 1993, https://www.icr.org/article/did-jonah-really-get-swallowed-by-whale.
12. Kenneth Boa and John Alan Turner, *The 52 Greatest Stories of the Bible* (Grand Rapids, MI: Baker Books, 2008), 41.

CHAPTER 2: BUT MAYBE DON'T START AT THE VERY BEGINNING
13. Mark L. Ward Jr., "How to Choose a Bible Translation That's Right for You," *Bible Study Magazine*, September/October 2019, http://www.biblestudy magazine.com/septoct-2019-article-3.
14. Some people argue that the KJV isn't as literal as its admirers purport, so it may fit better at a different location on this metaphorical table. It's a playful and flexible metaphorical buffet, so you can move it to a different place, if you'd like. For more on this, see https://carm.org/KJVO/is-the-kjv-the-most -literal-translation/; https://danielbwallace.com/2012/10/08/fifteen-myths -about-bible-translation/; and https://bloggingtheword.com/the-blog/the -less-than-literal-kjv.
15. Teresa Swanstrom Anderson, *Saying Yes in the Darkness: 7 Weeks in the Book of Psalms* (Colorado Springs: NavPress, 2020), 5.

CHAPTER 3: MODERN-DAY PSALMIST
16. John 6:67-68.
17. Martin Luther, *Preface to the Psalter*, accessible here: http://www.wolfmueller .co/wp-content/uploads/2018/02/Prefaces-to-the-Books-of-the-Bible-with -cover.pdf.
18. Psalm 5:1-2, NLT. Emphasis mine.
19. Psalm 6:2-3, NLT.
20. Psalm 6:6-7, NLT.
21. Psalm 10:12, 14.
22. Psalm 18:4-6. Emphasis mine.
23. Psalm 55:23, EHV.
24. Psalm 71:14, NLT.
25. Psalm 55:6-8.
26. Psalm 13:1-2.
27. Psalm 143:8, NLT.
28. Psalm 34:18.
29. Psalm 13:5-6, NLT.
30. Psalm 27:7-8.

CHAPTER 4: HOW IS THIS "A FUTURE AND A HOPE"?
31. Malachi 2:16, author's paraphrase.
32. Andy Stanley, *Irresistible: Reclaiming the New Jesus Unleashed for the World* (Grand Rapids, MI: Zondervan, 2018), 100.
33. Exodus 23:19. For more on why some Jews eat dairy and meat separately, see https://www.gotquestions.org/Jews-kosher-dairy-meat.html.
34. Exodus 31:14.
35. Leviticus 19:19.
36. Anderson, *Saying Yes in the Darkness*, 11.
37. John 16:33.
38. Stanley, *Irresistible*, 165.

39. John 13:34.
40. Galatians 5:6.
41. Trent Hunter and Stephen Wellum, *Christ from Beginning to End: How the Full Story of Scripture Reveals the Full Glory of Christ* (Grand Rapids, MI: Zondervan, 2018), 45–46.

CHAPTER 5: AFTER THE EARTHQUAKE

42. Micah 6:8.
43. Job 9:33, author's paraphrase.
44. 1 Timothy 2:5, author's paraphrase.
45. Job 14:14, author's paraphrase.
46. John 11:25, NLT.
47. Job 16:21, author's paraphrase.
48. Hebrews 9:24, NLT.
49. Job 19:7, author's paraphrase.
50. Job 19:25, NLT.
51. Hebrews 7:24-25, NLT.

CHAPTER 6: WHEN I DIDN'T KNOW

52. Leviticus 19:14, NLT.
53. Leviticus 19:30, NLT.
54. Leviticus 19:32, NLT.
55. Leviticus 19:19, NLT.
56. Leviticus 19:27, NLT.
57. Acts 2:22-23, 36, author's paraphrase.
58. Acts 3:17, NLT.
59. Proverbs 14:12, NLT.
60. 1 Corinthians 13:12, NLT.
61. Acts 3:19-20, NLT.
62. Philippians 2:3.
63. 1 Corinthians 16:14.
64. Philippians 2:3, NLT.
65. Hebrews 13:1.
66. Galatians 5:13, NLT. See also Philippians 2:3 and 1 Peter 4:9, 5:5.
67. Mark 9:50.
68. Romans 15:7.
69. Colossians 3:13, NLT.
70. Hebrews 10:24, NLT.
71. Anne Lamott, *Bird by Bird: Some Instructions on Writing and Life* (New York: Anchor Books, 2019), 146.
72. John 8:1-11.
73. John 8:7, NLT.
74. John 8:10-11, NLT.

CHAPTER 7: IMAGINE THAT DINNER TABLE
75. John 2:3-5, NLT.
76. John 2:6, NLT.
77. Luke 7:37, NLT.
78. *NLT Chronological Life Application Study Bible* (Carol Stream, IL: Tyndale, 2012), 1340 (commentary on Luke 7:38).
79. Matthew 14.
80. *NLT Chronological Life Application Study Bible*, 1289 (commentary on Mark 1:4).
81. Luke 22:54-62. See also Matthew 26:69-75; Mark 14:66-72; and John 18:17, 25-27.
82. John 21:7.
83. John 18:4-6, NLT.
84. Numbers 12:3, MEV.
85. John 13:23, NLT.
86. John 20:4, NLT.
87. John 20:15.
88. Phileena Heuertz, *Mindful Silence: The Heart of Christian Contemplation* (Downers Grove, IL: IVP Books, 2018), 50.

CHAPTER 8: EVEN IF HE DOESN'T
89. Matthew 17:20.
90. Matthew 9:20-22.
91. Eugene H. Peterson, *A Long Obedience in the Same Direction: Discipleship in an Instant Society* (Downers Grove, IL: IVP Books, 2019).
92. Matthew 20:1-16.
93. John 11:3, NLT.
94. John 12:3, NLT.
95. John 11:4, NLT.
96. Psalm 91:9-10, NLT.
97. John 11:5-6, NLT.
98. John 11:21-22, NLT.
99. John 11:32, NLT.
100. John 11:33, 35, NLT.
101. Stevie Swift, Facebook post, January 25, 2021, https://www.facebook.com/photo.php?fbid=242667767436188&set=p.242667767436188&type=3.
102. The tallest part of the White House is seventy feet high (https://www.whitehousehistory.org/press-room-old/white-house-dimensions). According to Daniel 3:1, Nebuchadnezzar's idol was sixty cubits high, which is approximately ninety feet (https://www.convertunits.com/from/cubit/to/feet).
103. Daniel 3:15, NLT.
104. Daniel 3:16-18, NLT. Emphasis mine.
105. Joshua 24:14-15.

106. Philippians 4:6.
107. Psalm 51:12, CEV.
108. Mark 9:24.

CHAPTER 9: IN THE MARGINS OF YOUR ACTUAL DAYS

109. Catherine McNiel, *Long Days of Small Things: Motherhood as a Spiritual Discipline* (Colorado Springs: NavPress, 2017).
110. Bekah DiFelice said this to me in a private conversation. Used with permission. You'll find more nuggets of wisdom in her book *Almost There: Searching for Home in a Life on the Move* (Colorado Springs: NavPress, 2017).
111. McNiel, *Long Days*, 7.
112. I heard her say it from the stage at a Living Proof event.
113. Lamott, *Bird by Bird*, 125–126.

CHAPTER 10: FEAR

114. Max Lucado, *Traveling Light: Releasing the Burdens You Were Never Intended to Bear* (Nashville: Thomas Nelson, 2013), 49.
115. Psalm 46:10.
116. *Rock and strong fortress*: Psalm 18:2; *Close to the brokenhearted*: Psalm 34:18; *With me in this moment*: Joshua 1:9; Matthew 1:23, 28:20.
117. Philippians 2:9-11.
118. 2 Corinthians 10:5.
119. Exodus 16:15-16, NLT.
120. Exodus 16:4.
121. Exodus 16:17-18, NLT.
122. Psalm 40:13.
123. Psalm 23:3.
124. Psalm 41:4.
125. Psalm 119:35; Job 28:20, 23.
126. Psalm 27:7.
127. Habakkuk 3:2.
128. Psalm 75:1.
129. Psalm 118:21.
130. Psalm 79:13.
131. Psalm 138:1.
132. Revelation 11:17.

CHAPTER 11: WORSHIP

133. It's true that we don't know for sure what type of fruit Eve and Adam ate; see https://answersingenesis.org/adam-and-eve/was-the-forbidden-fruit-an-apple/.
134. Exodus 15:20-21.
135. Joshua 6:20.
136. 1 Samuel 16:23; 1 Chronicles 15:16.
137. See the book of Psalms, many of which David wrote.

138. 1 Samuel 16.
139. *Sang a hymn*: Mark 14:26; *sang in jail*: Acts 16:25.

CHAPTER 12: TOGETHER WORK

140. This retelling of the event quotes directly from Mark 6:37-38, NLT and John 6:5, 9, 11, NLT; see also Matthew 14 and Luke 9.
141. *NLT Chronological Life Application Study Bible* (Carol Stream, IL: Tyndale, 2012), 1363.
142. If you're wondering about the differences between this and the account of Jesus being anointed that was referenced earlier, see https://answersingenesis .org/contradictions-in-the-bible/how-many-times-was-jesus-anointed/.
143. Matthew 26:12, NLT.
144. Exodus 35:31, NLT.
145. Exodus 26:1-6, NLT.
146. Matthew 27:50-51, NLT.
147. 1 Samuel 17:32-37, NLT.
148. Luke 1:38, NLT.

CHAPTER 13: QUICKSAND

149. Luke 23:43.
150. 2 Chronicles 6:32-33, NLT.
151. Exodus 12:31-42, NLT.
152. Romans 10:20, NLT; see also Isaiah 65:1.
153. Romans 9:25-26, NLT; see also Hosea 2:23.
154. Acts 9:1-31.
155. John 4:1-42.
156. John 3:1-21.
157. John 19:39, NLT.
158. John 19:38-42.

FIFTEEN THINGS TO KNOW AS YOU NAVIGATE THE BIBLE

159. Timothy Keller, *Prayer: Experiencing Awe and Intimacy with God* (New York: Penguin Books, 2014), 93.

ACKNOWLEDGMENTS

160. Emily Nagoski and Amelia Nagoski, *Burnout: The Secret to Unlocking the Stress Cycle* (New York: Ballantine Books, 2020), 35.